MW00935309

Baylor

Daily Devotions For Die-Hard Kids

Bears

Baylor

TO PARENTS/GUARDIANS FROM THE AUTHOR

DAILY DEVOTIONS FOR DIE-HARD KIDS is an adaptation of our DAILY DEVOTIONS FOR DIE-HARD FANS series. It is suggested for children ages 6 to 12, but that guideline is, of course, flexible. Only the parents or other adults can appraise the spiritual maturity of their children.

The devotions are written with the idea that a parent or adult will join the children to act as a mentor and spiritual guide for each devotion and the discussion that may ensue. The devotions seek to engage the child by capitalizing on his or her interest in the particular collegiate team the family follows. The interest in college sports is thus an oblique and somewhat tricky way, if you will, to lead your children to reading the Bible and learning about God, Jesus, and faith.

Each devotion contains a short Bible reading (except for occasional longer stories that must be read in their entirety), a paraphrase of the most pertinent scripture verse, a true Baylor sports story, and a theological discussion that ties everything together through a common theme. The devotion then concludes with a suggested activity that is based on the theme of the day. I tie each day's theological message to a child's life by referring to such aspects as school, household chores, video games, and relations with parents, siblings, and teachers, etc.

The devotions are intended to be fun for both the adult and the child, but they are also intended to be attempts to spark interest in quite serious matters of faith and living a godly life. A point of emphasis throughout the book is to impress upon the child that faith is not just for the times when the family gathers for formal worship in a particular structure, but rather is for every moment of every day wherever he or she may be.

Our children are under attack by the secular world as never before. It is a time fraught with danger for the innocence and the faith of our most precious family members. I pray that this book will provide your children with a better understanding of what it means to be a Christian. I also pray that this book will help lay the foundation for what will be a lifelong journey of faith for your children. May God bless you and your family.

ED MCMINN

Bears

Daily Devotions for Die-Hard Kids: Baylor Bears

Manufactured in the United States of America.

To order books or for more information, visit us at www.die-hardfans.com

Cover design by John Powell and Slynn McMinn;
Interior design by Slynn McMinn

DAILY DEVOTIONS FOR DIE-HARD FANS

ACC
CLEMSON TIGERS
DUKE BLUE DEVILS
FSU SEMINOLES
GA. TECH YELLOW JACKETS
NORTH CAROLINA TAR HEELS
NC STATE WOLFPACK
VIRGINIA CAVALIERS
VIRGINIA TECH HOKIES

BIG 12
BAYLOR BEARS
OKLAHOMA SOONERS
OKLAHOMA STATE COWBOYS
TCU HORNED FROGS
TEXAS LONGHORNS
TEXAS TECH RED RAIDERS

BIG 10
MICHIGAN WOLVERINES
OHIO STATE BUCKEYES
PENN STATE NITTANY LIONS

SEC
ALABAMA CRIMSON TIDE
MORE ALABAMA CRIMSON TIDE
ARKANSAS RAZORBACKS
AUBURN TIGERS
MORE AUBURN TIGERS
FLORIDA GATORS
GEORGIA BULLDOGS
MORE GEORGIA BULLDOGS
KENTUCKY WILDCATS
LSU TIGERS
MISSISSIPPI STATE BULLDOGS
MISSOURI TIGERS
OLE MISS REBELS
SOUTH CAROLINA GAMECOCKS
MORE S. CAROLINA GAMECOCKS
TEXAS A&M AGGIES
TENNESSEE VOLUNTEERS

NASCAR

DAILY DEVOTIONS FOR DIE-HARD KIDS

ALABAMA CRIMSON TIDE; BAYLOR BEARS; AUBURN TIGERS;
GEORGIA BULLDOGS; TEXAS LONGHORNS; TEXAS A&M AGGIES

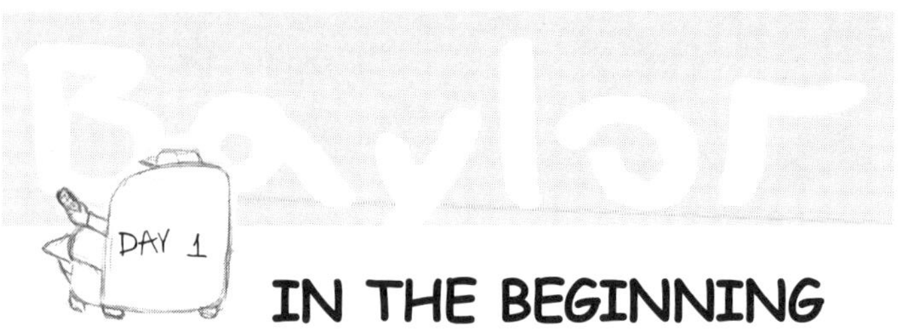

IN THE BEGINNING

Read Genesis 1:1; 2:1-3.

In the beginning, God created the heavens and the earth.

It was called "rugby modified," but it was the beginning of Baylor football.

On Thanksgiving Day in 1895, Baylor's first football game happened. It was really just some students horsing around. It featured the men of Georgia Burleson Hall playing members of the R.C.B. Calliopeans Club (whatever in the world that was). Burleson won 24-4. The game wasn't even called football; instead, it was something called "rugby modified."

In 1896, some Baylor students asked the faculty to allow a football team to play against other colleges. The faculty said no way.

But the teachers couldn't stop the students from playing among themselves, so they did. Those games among the students became so popular that the faculty allowed a team in 1899. Baylor's first true football squad went 2-1-1 with two games against Toby's Business College and games against Texas A&M and TCU. The loss was to A&M.

Those beginning games were played on campus at an area called the West End. The first mascot was a Bulldog; it was soon dropped.

Beginnings are important, but how we use those beginnings is even more important. You get a new beginning in your life every time the sun comes up and brings you a new day.

Have you ever thought that every morning is a gift from God? Well, it is. This present of a new day shows God's love for you. Each new day is full of promise. You can use it to make some wrong things right and to do some good.

How you use your new day is up to you. You should just make sure you walk with God all day long.

Try starting each morning by thanking God for the day and asking him to protect and lead you all day long.

THINGS HAPPEN

Read Isaiah 55:8-11.

God's thoughts are not like ours;
God's ways are different from ours.

Things happen to athletes all the time during the games they play. But going blind in one eye? It happened to a Baylor basketball player.

The Hustle and Courage Award given each year to a women's basketball player is named for Melissa Jones. Her No. 5 jersey has been retired. She was the 2011 Big 12 Conference Female Sportsperson of the Year. She was an All-Big 12 player.

But there's more to her story than just being a really good player whom everyone loved and admired. She was a senior in 2011, and against Oklahoma, she dived for a loose ball and hit her head on the court. During the next few minutes, the vision in her right eye faded to complete blackness. She still played the rest of the game.

Her sight didn't return, but she didn't stop. She missed only one game, playing the rest of the season with protective sunglasses.

And she never complained about the awful thing that had happened to her. She just thanked God for letting her play on. "It's part of my life now," she said, "and I just have to adapt to it."

Things happen to you, too, don't they? Maybe when it started raining just as you were set to go swimming. Or the time you got real sick, and the doctor had to give you a shot.

You don't know why stuff like that happens. The truth is God doesn't tell us why. His ways are different from ours. After all, he is God and we are not. So we don't know what's going to happen next. It catches us by surprise.

God just asks that we trust him. He is the one in charge, and everything will be all right for those who trust in Jesus.

List three things that happened to you that you really don't know why they did.

GIFT-WRAPPED

Read James 1:16-18.

Every good and perfect gift comes from God.

Players at a bowl game get really nice gifts these days. One time, though, the Bears got — well, something really cheap.

In the 1950s, Baylor went to the Orange, Gator, and Sugar Bowls. Then came 1961 and something called the Gotham Bowl.

Injuries wiped out the Bears that season. They struggled to a 5-5 record. The sponsors of a new bowl in New York City were desperate for a team to play there. They had tried to start the bowl the season before and couldn't find two teams to play. So they asked the Bears to come up north. Baylor accepted and beat Utah State 24-9.

The bowl had a lot of problems because the people running it didn't really know what they were doing. At the last minute, someone let them know they were supposed to have gifts for the teams. So they came up with a really special gift for everyone: a shoeshine kit.

Opening gifts on Christmas or your birthday is fun and exciting, especially when it's something you really want.

But maybe you've learned a surprising little truth: It's fun to give gifts, too. Making people you love happy makes you happy.

But no matter how many gifts you give, you can't top the greatest gift-giver of them all: God. That's because all the good things in your life come from God. Friends at school, family, love, good health, the air you breathe, the sun, your life itself — they're all gifts from God. He even gave you eternal life through the gift of his son.

So what in the world can you give God in return? Your love and your life.

Cut out a paper heart and decorate it.
Put your name on it.
Then gift-wrap it as a gift to God.

TALK THE TALK

Read Mark 16:14-16.

Jesus told the disciples, "Go everywhere and preach the good news to everyone."

The recruit wasn't sure Baylor was right for him. After all, he couldn't understand half of what the head coach said to him.

Danny Watkins came to Baylor in 2008 from a junior college. He was big and strong, but he hadn't played much football. He was Canadian and grew up playing hockey and rugby.

His first talk with head coach Art Briles left him confused, but it had nothing to do with football. He said he talked on the phone with the coach for about 30 minutes. "I don't think I understood half of what he said. I'm not sure he understood me either," he said.

But Watkins came to Waco anyway. At his first practices, the coaches praised him and kept telling him, "Good job, Danny! That dog will hunt!" Confused, Watkins tapped a teammate on the shoulder and asked, "Where's this dog they keep talking about?"

Despite the language problems, he was a two-year starter for the Bears. He was taken in the first round of the 2011 NFL draft.

You take it for granted that when you talk to somebody at school, they will understand you. But how awful would it be if your teachers didn't understand a word you said?

Now think about this. All over the world people speak different languages; they can't talk to each other. But billions of those people from all the countries of the world are giving their lives to Jesus. They are becoming Christians. How cool is that?

You see, everybody in the world has words for hope, love, joy, and God. And Jesus speaks those words better than anybody else, no matter what language they're spoken in.

Learn the word for "hello" in three foreign languages. At school, say hello to someone in them. See what happens.

YOU DECIDE

Read James 1:5-8.

A person who doubts God can never decide what to do.

Robert Griffin III — Baylor's greatest football player ever — had decided where he was going to play college ball. And it wasn't Waco.

Baylor's official athletic site calls Griffin "a once-in-a-generation" athlete who "lifted Baylor to decades-high heights." The site says Griffin became the face of the Baylor football program. Yet, in high school, the 2011 Heisman-Trophy winner decided he would play for Houston and not Baylor.

Griffin wanted to play quarterback in college. Some schools wanted him to play defensive back or receiver. Boy, was that wrong! When Baylor recruited him, the coaches told him he could play quarterback only if he walked on for that position. Griffin said forget it.

Bears

He decided to play for Houston and its head coach, Art Briles, who told him he could play quarterback. Then in November, Baylor's head coach was fired and Briles replaced him. Griffin decided to follow Briles to Baylor.

The rest is glorious Bear history.

Most of the decisions in your life are made for you, aren't they? Your parents, your grandparents, your teachers, and maybe even your babysitter — they decide things for you.

So when you do get the chance to make a decision, you don't want to mess it up. How can you make a good decision? It isn't always easy Sometimes deciding what to do is hard. So what do you do?

You talk it over with your parents. You pray about it with them. You look in the Bible with them to see if God has a word about the choice you face. When you know what God's answer is, you do it. When you obey God, you can know that you are doing the right thing.

Make a list of the decisions you will make tomorrow. Go ahead and pray for God's help in making them.

THE PROPHET

Isaiah 53:6-9.

He went like a lamb to the slaughter and said not a word.

Terrance Ganaway made a prophet out of head coach Art Briles.

Ganaway is one of the greatest running backs in Baylor football history. As a senior in 2011, he set thirteen school records.

As the season began, though, Ganaway wasn't sure he even wanted to play football anymore. His whole time at Baylor had been disappointing. When fall practice began, he wasn't listed as the starter. But the coaches told him he could be the team's starter if he worked hard and got ready. He did.

Heading into the Missouri game, the Bears were only 4-3. Each day of the week before the game, Briles told Ganaway he was going to have a big game against Missouri. "It's going to be a big week for you, G-Way," the coach said. "Do you feel it? You should."

Briles did indeed make a prophet out of his head coach. (A prophet is someone who tells something about the future.) He ran for 186 yards and two touchdowns. One of them was an 80-yard run. Baylor won a thriller 42-39.

The Bears did not lose another game.

In the Old Testament, you read a lot about God's prophets. Isaiah was one. Did these guys walk around predicting the future? Well, not really.

Instead, they delivered a word that God had given them. Sometimes — as when Isaiah spoke of Jesus' suffering and death — that involved the future. But typically, the prophets told the people what God wanted them to do, how God said they should live.

Where is your prophet? How can you find out what God wants you to do? You read the Bible and you pray. It's all right there for you.

Write down five predictions (like your next test grade). Check them later to see how many you got right.

HUGS AND KISSES

Read John 15:9-14.

Jesus said, "I have loved you. Now remain in my love."

Felix Obi had done enough jumping. So instead of jumping for joy, he settled for hugs to celebrate his national championship.

A sophomore, Obi entered the 2014 NCAA Indoor Track and Field Championships as the favorite in the triple jump. He was in trouble, though, before he even started.

He had some serious knee problems that meant he was in bad pain every time he jumped. He fouled on his first try and wound up in fourth place after his second jump.

Then came the biggest jump of Obi's career. He soared more than 54 feet to break his own school record by six inches. That leap left him in first place. It also finished off his knee. He could only stand around and wait to see if

Bears

anybody outjumped him. Nobody did.

"It was amazing, considering he only took three jumps," said head coach Todd Harbour.

"I almost wanted to cry when I was out there," Obi said. "I just couldn't believe it, until the last jump was done."

Since his knee wouldn't let him jump anymore, Obi shared a lot of hugs with his coaches and teammates to celebrate his victory.

A hug is a sign of affection. When you hug someone, you're showing them you care for them. It doesn't just make them feel good; it makes you feel good, too. A hug is also a symbol. When you hold someone close, it says how closely you hold them in your heart.

The greatest hugger of them all is God. Through Jesus, God tries to pull us closer to him because he loves us. A good hug takes two, so God always wants us to hug him back.

We do that by loving Jesus. To love Jesus is to hug God — and that feels mighty good.

Do you like to hug people? Think of some folks you'd like to hug and then do it the next time you see them.

GOOD JOB!

Read Matthew 25:14-21.

The boss said, "Good job, good and faithful worker."

Talk about doing a good job! In 2011-12, Baylor's athletes had the best year in the history of college athletics.

During that school year, Baylor's "big-time" sports of football, men's and women's basketball, and baseball rolled up 129 wins. That's the most in major college history.

Get this! From Nov. 1. to Jan. 16, the football and basketball teams were 40-0. Those three sports combined for 80 wins, an all-time college record.

Baylor's athletic director said, "This was the year the unbelievable became believable at Baylor." To top it off, Robert Griffin III won the Heisman Trophy.

The football team went 10-3 and won its

Bears

bowl game. The men's basketball team went 30-8. The women won the national title with a 40-0 record. The baseball team won 24 games in a row and went to the playoffs.

But there was more. All nineteen teams the school fielded made the postseason! That means they were among the best teams in all of college sports.

In 2011-12, Baylor's teams did a good job.

Good job. Way to go. It's nice hearing those words, isn't it? Whether you've aced a test, helped out with a church play, or finished a science project. When you work hard, you like to have people notice and tell you.

The most important "good job" of all is the one that comes from God. As a Christian, you will meet God in Heaven one day. You will want God to say to you, "Well done. Good job."

Nothing else in life is as important as doing a good job for God. You do that by always doing your best and by always giving him the glory when you do it.

Name some ways that you do a good job for God.

CELEBRATION TIME

Read Luke 15:8-10.

Heaven celebrates every time a sinner turns away from his sin.

The quarterback cried, a safety brought out some Tostitos, the fans rushed the field, and the team was handed a shiny new trophy. Hey, now that's a celebration!

The Texas game of 2013 was only four minutes old when the crowd at Floyd Casey Stadium got some big news. Oklahoma had beaten Oklahoma State. That meant Baylor and the Longhorns were playing for the Big 12 championship.

The Bears won going away 30-10. They were champs of the Big 12 for the first time.

Before the game ended, the fans chanted "B-C-S" for the big-time bowl the team would be playing in. When the game ended, many of the fans ran onto the field. They wanted to celebrate with the players.

Quarterback Bryce Petty collapsed in tears. "I don't do that much," he said. Safety Ahmad Dixon showed up with two bags of Tostitos to celebrate going to the Fiesta Bowl. The league boss presented the championship trophy.

It was a wild and fun-filled celebration.

Have you ever whooped and hollered when Baylor scored a touchdown? Or maybe you just smiled and felt good inside the first time you got a hit in a softball or a baseball game.

When we're happy about something that just happened or something we did, we celebrate. We celebrate special days, too; days like your birthday or Easter Sunday.

Did you know God and the angels celebrate, too? They sing and shout and throw a party quite often. They celebrate every time someone accepts Jesus as their savior.

Just think. When you said "yes" to Jesus, you made the angels dance.

What did you do to celebrate your last birthday? Why does your family celebrate Christmas?

GOOD-BYE

Read John 13:33-36.

Jesus told Peter, "Where I am going, you can't follow now."

After 64 seasons, the Bears said good-bye to Floyd Casey Stadium in 2013. They moved into the dazzling McLane Stadium on the Brazos. Once upon a time, though, the old Bears' den was something to see.

"You're dadgum right we wanted to play in the new stadium," said linebacker Gale Galloway. "Here was a fabulous football field with no track around it." He was talking about the place called Baylor Stadium; it was renamed Floyd Casey Stadium in 1989.

The truth is that "the Baylor players had never seen anything this grand in their city." Their old field had wooden stands that held only 15,000 people. "When the wind blew, those wooden stadiums would sway," said

Terry Downs, who played from 1947-50. "It was a big step going to the new stadium."

The team moved into its new home in 1950. "We could hardly believe it," Galloway said.

Now that old place, too, is part of the past.

Even though you're a youngster, you have probably known good-byes — and they hurt. Maybe your best friend moved away. Maybe you moved away and had to tell a whole lot of your friends and buddies good-bye. It's sad to stand and wave while your grandparents drive off on their way home after a visit.

Jesus knows just how you feel. He always had his friends around him, but it came time for him to tell them good-bye. He was going away; he would leave them.

But Jesus wasn't just moving to another town. He was about to finish his mission on Earth. He would provide a way so that none of us would ever have to say good-bye again.

List some people you have said good-bye to. Get their addresses from a parent and write them a note.

HEAD GAMES

Read Job 28:20-28.

Respect God, which will show that you are wise.

Baylor head football coach Art Briles was smart enough to talk about horse ranches and Cadillacs. It helped him keep a star player.

In 2007, the head Bear knew that star tackle John Smith was ready to go to the NFL. Briles learned that Smith was really big into horses and ranching. He also loved his grandmother.

He met with Smith and told him if he left Baylor, he would be drafted in the middle rounds. That meant he wouldn't get as much money.

Then the coach said what he had carefully thought out. "If you stay," he said, "[you'll see] there's a big difference between visiting the ranch and owning the ranch. . . . You can either buy your grandmother a car or a Cadillac."

The head coach was right and Smith knew

Bears

it. He stayed and was All-America in 2008. He landed a contract for $33 million. He bought two things right off: a Cadillac for his grandmother and a big horse ranch for himself.

Being smart is one of God's gifts. No matter what's happening, you can always use your brain to be smart and make good decisions.

Have you noticed that you use your brain all the time every day? In every class at school, you have to use your brain so you'll be smarter.

The same thing applies to your faith in God and Jesus. When you go to church or open your Bible, you need to keep on thinking. You seek Jesus with everything you have: your heart, your soul, your body, and your mind.

There's nothing strange about using your brain to think about God. That's because God gave you your brain to begin with. That means he likes people to be smart.

For God, loving him and trusting in Jesus is the smartest thing of all.

Open your Bible at random and read a few verses. Use your brain to figure out what they mean as best you can.

CHOICES

Read Deuteronomy 30:15-16, 19.

I'm offering you the choice of life or death.

Two choices decided Chris McAllister's football career in college. He got to make one but the other one was made for him.

Right before Christmas in 2008, McAllister chose Baylor as the school where he would play college ball. Some of his buddies thought he'd lost his mind. After all, it had been years since Baylor had even been to a bowl game.

"I trusted in Coach [Art] Briles," McAllister said. The coach convinced him that Baylor was about to become a winner.

McAllister started at linebacker in 2010. In January 2011, the new defensive coach called him into his office and told him he was moving to defensive end. McAllister had no choice in the decision, but he didn't want to do it. He liked playing linebacker at Baylor, but he went along with the move for the good of the team.

It was a great choice. McAllister became a star. He was twice All-Big 12 First Team. He played on four bowl teams and a Big-12 champ.

You can choose what ice cream flavor you want. Maybe what to wear to school. What movie to see. What you want for your birthday or Christmas. What friends you have.

Right now, though, your choices are limited by your age. One day, you will be grown up. What kind of life you have will be decided by the choices you make. What kind of work to do. Where to live. What friends you choose.

The most important choice you will ever make — whether a kid or a grown-up — has to do with faith. Do you choose to love God and follow Jesus? Or not.

God said choosing his way is life. To choose against him is to choose death. Life or death. What kind of choice is that?

List some choices you will get to make tomorrow. Then check back and see if you made them. And what you chose.

SMILING FACES

Read Isaiah 35:5-10.

Those who find Jesus will also find joy that lasts forever.

Nichole Jones often smiled at those she met at the starting line — right before she left them eating her dust.

Jones is one of the greatest runners in Baylor history. From 2006-2010, she was All-America multiple times and set several school records.

Early on, Jones saw she was an athlete. But she couldn't figure out how to use her skills. She was cut from her middle school volleyball team. When she made her school's basketball team, her coach told her to stand still on the court so she wouldn't mess up!

Running didn't start out too well either. She ran a two-mile race one time and was lapped twice. The next year she was lapped only once.

She kept getting better. She was confident

she would because of her faith in Christ, not faith in her talent. "I'm running to be a witness for God," she said.

The joy of her faith showed in her running. That's where the smile came in. She wore it while she left others behind. Her Baylor coach named her "The Smiling Assassin."

A smile is simply a wonderful thing. When you smile at someone, it makes them want to smile back at you. That's the way a smile works. It seems to make everybody around you happy, like turning on a bright light in a dark room.

And, hey, you have a good reason to walk around with a goofy smile on your face all the time. Not because of a joke you've heard or from anything you've done but because of what God has done for you. God loves you so much that he gave you Jesus so you could live with him in Heaven one day.

Now that's something to smile about!

Stand in front of a mirror and make some different smiles. How did you feel? How does your smile make others feel?

DRY RUN

Read 1 Kings 16:29-30; 17:1; 18:1.

Elijah told Ahab, "There won't be any rain for the next few years."

The drought lasted sixteen years. Even the weather helped to stretch it out.

Baylor's 2010 football team had as its goal to get to a bowl game. After all, the Bears had not played in one since 1994.

Robert Griffin III had recovered from the knee injury that had put him on the bench in 2009. The squad looked to be in good shape to get the six wins it needed for a bowl.

Sure enough, the Bears jumped out to a 5-2 record with Kansas State coming to town. They played a wild game and Baylor won 47-42. Because the win made the Bears bowl eligible, it was called "the biggest win for the program in more than a decade."

To win, the Bears had to battle both K-State

and the weather. Lightning forced a delay of 107 minutes before the game started. "Man, it really is that hard to be bowl eligible at Baylor," head coach Art Briles joked.

He could joke because the drought was over.

If you live in Texas, you know a little something about drought, don't you? It gets really hot down here. Sometimes in the summer you probably don't get a whole lot of rain in your hometown.

The sun bakes everything, including the concrete that gets so hot it burns your feet. Ever seen a truck with "Wash Me" written on the back windshield?

God put in you a physical thirst for water to keep you alive. But he also put a spiritual thirst in you. Without God, we are like a dried-up pond. There's no life, only death.

There's only one fountain to go to and drink all you want of the true water of life: Jesus.

Fill an empty water bottle with sand to remind you how a soul looks without God: all dried up and dead.

PRAYER WARRIORS

Read Luke 18:1-5.

Jesus told his disciples a story to show them they should always pray and never give up.

Doctors gave Mariah Chandler up for dead. Then her mother prayed.

As a graduate student in 2013-14, Chandler ended her Baylor career as a part-time starter for the women's basketball team. The way she looked at life was rare for one so young. She played each game and lived each day truly thankful for all her blessings.

That's because when she was 7 years old, she died. Doctors found that she had a heart problem, and she went into the hospital for surgery. The surgical team couldn't revive her. They pronounced her dead.

Mariah's mother walked into the room to see her daughter's body, but she did more.

Bears

She started to pray, begging God for a miracle, asking God to save her daughter. Suddenly, Mariah's heart monitor started beeping.

Doctors had no way to explain it. The only explanation was the real one: God had stepped in and answered a faithful woman's prayer.

Jesus told us that we should always pray and never give up as Mariah Chandler's mother did. But what is the right way to pray? Do you have to get on your knees? Can you be by yourself, or do you have to be in church? Should you pray out loud or can you whisper?

The truth is there is no right or wrong way to pray. What counts is that you pray, and that you mean it from your heart. Here's another truth: God hears every one of your prayers.

Sometimes — and we don't know why — God doesn't answer prayers right away. Sometimes God's answer is "no." But he knows what's best for you even when you don't.

No matter what, you keep praying.

Talk about the last time God answered one of your prayers.

GOOD ADVICE

Read Isaiah 9:6-7.

A son will be given to us, and he will be called Wonderful Adviser.

Art Briles had some advice for his quarterback, but it wasn't what he expected. It had to do with his hair.

In the spring of 2012, RGIII was gone. Nick Florence was the next Baylor quarterback.

But the head Bear still had some advice for his senior leader. He called him to the weight room before spring practice began.

The coach told Florence everybody thought of him as "this pretty boy who's perfect and doesn't make mistakes." He told Florence "to dirty it up." He advised his quarterback to let his beard and his hair grow out.

Florence thought his coach was kidding until he got a text that night. It had a picture of Snoop Dogg and Martha Stewart cooking in a kitchen. The coach wrote, "One of these is a convicted felon." (Ask a parent what this had to do with shaggy hair and neatness.)

Florence got the message. He avoided all clippers for several months. The advice and his new shaggy look may not have helped, but it sure didn't hurt. He set or tied eight school records in 2012.

Just about everybody tells you what to do. Your parents, your teachers, your coaches — they all order you around.

That's different from advice. You may get advice from your friends or classmates, from older kids or your brothers or sisters. They don't tell you what to do, but they may say you should dress, act, or talk a certain way.

The problem is you don't really know whether their advice is good or bad. Do you have a place that always gives you good advice?

Yes, you do. It's called the Bible. In it, God advises you on how you are to live. God's advice is always good; it will never hurt you.

Ask a parent for advice about how to handle a problem you have at school.

UNCERTAINTY

Read Psalm 18:1-2.

God is my rock and my fortress.

You would think folks would know for sure who won a college football game. Maybe not.

In the earliest days of Baylor football, the Bears sometimes played AddRan College three times a year. It's today's TCU and was in Waco then. They played so much because they didn't have to travel.

The second game of 1907 ended with no one certain about who won. The TCU record book shows an 11-10 win for the Horned Frogs. For years, however, the Baylor record book listed the game as a 10-9 win for the Bears.

The uncertainty happened because of a call late in the game. The refs couldn't agree about whether a Baylor ball carrier was tackled in his own end zone for a safety (two points).

The problem was the goal line. It had disappeared in all the dust and dirt. While the refs talked the matter over, the players and the fans "went home to supper with their own [ideas] about the final score."

Only after about a century did the schools agree the game was an 11-10 win for TCU.

You've been uncertain, haven't you? What about a hard test you had coming up? Or a dance recital or play? You got nervous because you didn't know how you would do.

Life is like that. You will always be uncertain about some things. That's because you may not know what's going on — like those Baylor fans in 1907 — or what will happen next.

So is there anything in your life that you can be certain about? Something or someone that will never let you down?

You can be certain about God. He is your rock. He is your fort. He will always be there for you, and he will never want anything but good for you. You can depend on God.

List some things you might be certain about in your life. Then talk about how maybe they could let you down.

GOOD NEWS

Read Matthew 28:1-10.

The angel said, "Jesus has risen, just as he said he would! Take a look at where he was buried."

On Nov. 17, 2012, college football fans and sportswriters all across the country were talking about the news out of Waco.

What was all the fuss about? The Bears had beaten the Kansas State Wildcats. So why was that such big news? After all, Baylor had beaten K-State before.

Well, the Wildcats went into the game 10-0, ranked No. 1, and had dreams of winning the national championship. The Bears were 4-5 and scrapping to land any kind of bowl berth.

So it was a fluke, right? The Bears just got lucky at the last minute. Nope — and that was part of the news. Baylor beat the daylights out of the Wildcats.

Bears

"All week we believed we were going to beat them," said quarterback Nick Florence. "We didn't want to be surprised when it happened."

Everyone else certainly was surprised by the news and the final score: A 52-24 beatdown.

It's lots of fun to get good news. Like when your teacher tells you that you made a good grade on a test. Or when your parents tell you that you're going to the beach.

People, especially grown-ups, get news all the time. Some of it's good; some of it's not. You've probably seen your mom or dad watching a news channel on TV.

News is about what's happening right now. That's why it's news. But here's something really strange. The biggest news story in the history of the world is almost two thousand years old!

The greatest and the best news story of all time happened the morning Jesus rose from the dead and walked out of his tomb. It's still today's news, the most important story of all.

Write a news story about something in the Bible. Read it to your parents.

PLAN AHEAD

Read Psalm 33:4-11.

The plans of the Lord stand firm forever.

Grant Teaff had a plan to help his team out, and it made the other team's coach really mad.

Teaff was Baylor's head football coach from 1972-92. He won more games than any other coach in the school's history.

In 1975, the Bears took on Michigan in Ann Arbor. More than 100,000 wild Wolverine fans would be cheering against them. So Teaff came up with a plan. He told his players that when they trotted onto the field, more than 100,000 people would be cheering for them.

Teaff had noticed that the visiting team always took the field first. Also, the teams entered the field through the same tunnel. So his plan was to let his team trot out after Michigan did while the fans were going nuts.

Bears

An angry Michigan coach said Baylor had to take the field when he said so. "It's not in the contract," Teaff said. "We'll follow you."

So they did. They got cheers from 104,000 Michigan fans and 248 Baylor fans. Teaff's plan certainly didn't hurt. Only a missed field goal kept the fired-up Bears from pulling off the upset. The game wound up tied at 14.

People make plans every single day. You do, too. You plan to go to school. You plan to do your chores. You plan to go spend some time with your grandparents.

But what if something happens to mess up your plans? What if you wake up sick and your plan to go to school doesn't work out? Sometimes even when you make a great plan, everything goes wrong, doesn't it?

God has plans for you, too. God's plan for you has nothing but good things like happiness, love, and kindness. But it will work only if you make God the boss of your life.

What are your plans for tomorrow? Tomorrow night, think back and see if they turned out the way you planned.

SMART MOVE

Read 1 Kings 4:29-31; 11:4.

Solomon was wise until he grew old and didn't follow God with all his heart anymore.

Baylor coach Art Briles looked like he was making a really dumb move. It turned out to be pretty smart after all.

In the third game of the 2009 season, RGIII tore his ACL and was out for the rest of the year. In the same game, backup quarterback Blake Szymanski hurt his shoulder. That left it up to Nick Florence. He would have a great season as a senior in 2012. Right then, though, he had barely taken any snaps at practice.

As he got better so did the team and its season. Against Missouri, he set a record by throwing for 427 yards. Baylor led 33-29 late in the game and was on Missouri's 1-yard line.

So it looked like a dumb move when Briles

Bears

pulled Florence out of the game. But the head coach wanted an extra blocker on the field. His jersey number was 11, and that was Florence's number, too. Having the two players on the field at the same time meant a penalty.

So it was a smart move. Especially when Terrance Ganaway scored. Baylor won 40-32.

Remember that time you left your homework lying on your desk at home? That cold morning you went to school without a jacket? The time your library book was overdue?

Just because we make some good grades in school doesn't mean we don't do some dumb things now and then. Plenty of smart people sometimes say and do things that aren't too smart. Like Solomon when he got old.

Some people even say that if you're really smart you can't believe in God. How dumb is that? Who do they think made us smart in the first place?

You got your brains and your smarts from God. Forgetting that isn't smart at all.

Talk about why it's smart to love God and follow Jesus.

PAYBACK

Read Matthew 5:38-45.

Jesus said to love those who don't like you and to pray for those who do you wrong.

The Bears had payback on their minds when they played Kansas State in 2013.

In 2011, Baylor was undefeated and ranked 15th in the nation when the team went to Manhattan to play K-State. "It was probably one of the loudest places we've ever played," said receiver Tevin Reese. The crowd noise bothered the Bears so much that they "couldn't hear themselves talk" in the fourth quarter. The Wildcats scored ten points late in the game to win 36-35.

Okay, now how weird is this? Two years later, the Bears were undefeated and ranked 15th when they went to Manhattan again. "We want to prove to people we can win on the road," Reese said. And get some payback.

But the crowd noise helped K-State to a 25-21 lead. Then early in the fourth quarter, Bryce Petty hit Reese with a 54-yard TD pass. Baylor went on to win 35-25. And get payback.

In Baylor's big rivalries, one team is always looking to pay the other team back for getting beat the last time. It's part of what makes college football so much fun.

But real life doesn't work that way. Should you get even when somebody does something wrong to you? Jesus said not to.

The reason is that paying somebody back only makes everything worse. It will make the other person want to pay you back and hurt you again. And so it keeps going. It's just a mess when you live like that.

Jesus said to do something much easier. Just forget it. Go on about your business. Go on with your life. It's more fun that way.

Talk to your parents about something wrong someone has done to you. What should you do about it?

RUN FOR IT

Read John 20:1-10.

Peter and the other disciple ran to Jesus' tomb.

Did you know this? Robert Griffin III didn't start out at Baylor playing football. He first ran track.

Since he made such good grades, Griffin graduated from high school early. He then started at Baylor in the spring of 2008 while the rest of his class was still in high school.

So the first uniform of the most famous football player in Baylor's history didn't have any pads. For his first college sports event, he wore a sprinter's suit. He ran hurdles that spring; his first college football season was the following fall.

RGIII traded track for football when spring practice began. After it ended, he ran track full time. He won the Big 12 championship in

Bears

the 400-meter hurdles and went on to the national championships where he placed third.

He tried out for the 2008 Olympics team but missed it by one spot. That was a good thing for Baylor football. "Had I qualified for the Olympics," Griffin said, "I might not have ever played football."

You probably do a lot of running. You run at recess and at PE. Spot a playground and you run to it without thinking. You run during a game, whether it's softball or basketball. You run a race to see who's the fastest.

But no matter how hard, how far, or how fast you run, you can never outrun God. He is always there with you. He wants you to run, too — right to Jesus. Life is like a long race, and the only way to win it is by running it step by step with Jesus.

Here's something odd. The best way to run to Jesus is to drop to your knees — and pray.

If it's not dark yet, go out and run around your home, picturing God running with you all the way.

I DIDN'T KNOW THAT!

Read John 8:31-34.

You will know the truth, and the truth will set you free.

Frank Broyles had no clue what was going on, and he had a hard time finding out.

Broyles went on to become a College Football Hall-of-Fame head coach at Arkansas. In 1949, he was a young assistant for Bob Woodruff at Baylor. The team went 8-2.

The highlight of the season was the SMU game. The Mustangs had won the conference title two times in a row. Baylor quarterback Adrian Burk, who led the nation in passing, threw an 80-yard TD pass to Dudley Parker on the game's first play.

Broyles was in the press box during the game. He left shortly before halftime to meet the team in the locker room. While the elevator crawled to the ground, he heard a huge roar from the crowd. When he reached the ground, he ran to the nearest fan and shouted, "What happened." "Those guys scored again," was the answer. Still clueless, Broyles had to ask, "Yes, yes, but which ones?"

It probably was Baylor. The Bears won 35-20.

When you don't know something, it's called ignorance. It doesn't mean you're too dumb to live; you just don't know it.

That's why you go to school. To learn things. There's a whole lot you don't know. Like how they get toothpaste into the tube. How they make paper from trees. How birds can sing.

You get along all right without knowing all that stuff, don't you? But it makes a big difference if you don't know about Jesus. In that case, ignorance sets you apart from God. So you read this book and you read the Bible and you go to Sunday school to help you learn about God and Jesus.

And that's worth knowing about!

Explain how not knowing Jesus is really a bad thing for people.

COMEBACK KIDS

Read Acts 9:18-22.

Those who heard Paul asked, "Isn't he the one who persecuted and killed Christians in Jerusalem?"

The 1980 Bears had to come back from a crushing loss, but they had an inspiration the likes of which they had never seen.

Baylor was 7-0 and ranked No. 10 when San Jose State upset them. Head coach Grant Teaff knew his team needed something to inspire them after the tough loss.

He made his weekly call to Kyle Woods. The season before, Woods had damaged his spine at a practice. He would never walk again. Teaff asked him to come to the game Saturday.

The locker room was dead quiet before the kickoff. Teaff hadn't planned to do it, but he asked Woods to speak to the team. "Guys, it's simple," Woods told them. "In life, setbacks have to be turned into comebacks."

Then he put his hands on his wheelchair and pushed himself to his feet. It was the first time he had stood since the accident. He would never stand again.

Inspired by Kyle Woods' glorious comeback, the Bears didn't lose another game.

A comeback means you come from behind. You know by now that you don't always win. You make an A on a test one day and sprain your ankle the next. You do all your chores at home but get in trouble for talking in class.

In life, even for a kid, winning isn't about never losing. Things will go wrong for you sometimes. Winning means you pick yourself up from your defeat and keep going. You make a comeback of your own.

Besides, God's grace is always there for you, so your comeback can always be bigger than your setback. With Jesus in your life, it's not how you start that counts; it's how you finish.

Remember a time a team you like made a comeback. Compare that to a time you came back when something went wrong.

STRANGE BUT TRUE

Read Philippians 2:5-11.

Jesus is God, but he became a servant and died on a cross.

It's strange but true: Baylor once played a softball game that took more than seven years to finish.

Baylor's first softball team was in 1974. The women played on through 1988, but then the decision was made to drop softball in favor of women's golf.

On April 27, the squad played Sam Houston State in what was to be the last Baylor softball game ever. The official record lists the game as a 7-2 Baylor loss. But that doesn't really tell the whole truth about this strange game.

With two outs in the bottom of the last inning, the Baylor team walked off the field. They did that to protest the decision and to show that Baylor women's softball wasn't over.

Bears

They were right. In 1994, the program was brought to life again in a one-of-a-kind way. With some members of that 1988 team at the game, Baylor and Sam Houston State began play with two outs in the last inning. Baylor scored a run to make the final score 7-3. The strange game was finished after seven years.

A lot of things about life are strange. Isn't it strange that you can't eat all the sugar you want to? Isn't it strange that you can't play all the time when everybody knows that's what kids are good at?

God's kind of strange, too, isn't he? He's the ruler of all the universe; he can do anything he wants to. And so he let himself be killed by a bunch of men who nailed him to two pieces of wood. Isn't that downright weird?

And why did God do it? That's strange, too. He did it because he loves you so much. In the person of Jesus, God died so you can live, so you can be with him one day in Heaven.

List five things about God that are strange (like "he never dies"). Tell why they're strange.

WELCOME HOME

Read 2 Corinthians 5:6-9.

We would really rather be out of our bodies and at home with God.

Waco and Baylor didn't seem like home to Levi Norwood. Then he realized they were the places his faith could grow the most.

From 2012-14, Norwood was a three-time starter at wide receiver and the team's leading kick returner. His dad was a coach who left Penn State in 2007 to join Art Briles at Baylor.

Levi wasn't happy about leaving his high school. "I got down here and the food was different, the people were different, the weather was different, the land — there's no mountains or hills here," he recalled.

He adjusted, but he didn't want to stay. In 2010, he signed with Penn State; he was on his way home again.

Or maybe not. Levi found something "that

was more important to me than going up to Penn State." Just what was it? He saw that the place that give him the best chance to grow his faith in Jesus was Baylor.

State released him and he stayed home.

When somebody says "home," what do you think about? A house? Your room? Your toys?

But home isn't just a place. More than walls and floors, a home is about people. You are at home when you are with the people you love and the people who love you. That's why it doesn't matter what you live in. What matters is the people you share it with, including God.

Oddly, as a Christian, you spend your whole life as a kid and as a grown-up away from your real home. That's because your real home is with God and Jesus in Heaven. There you will live forever with the people whom you love and who love you most of all.

You'll be home because you'll be with God, and nobody loves you more than God does.

List the different places you have lived. What was different about each one? What made them all feel like home?

TRICK PLAYS

Read Acts 19:11-16.

Some tricksters tried to use Jesus' name to drive out evil spirits. They wound up naked and bleeding.

The Bears once pulled a trick play on TCU that involved the uniform.

The Frogs led 8-6 at halftime of the game on Thanksgiving Day 1908. But then the Bears did something slightly unusual. Baylor's star left end, John Fouts, put on some blue stockings. Blue just happened to be a TCU color at the time. He kept on his gray Baylor jersey.

After halftime, Fouts took off his jersey to reveal a blue one underneath. It matched TCU's uniforms so well that when a play started, he mixed right in with TCU's players. They were totally confused.

TCU's players and coaches were upset at what they called a lowdown trick. Baylor's captain pointed out there was no rule against it.

The trick must have worked. The Bears outscored TCU 17-0 the last half to win 23-8. A news report of the game said the trick spread "bitterness and confusion" among TCU's team and its fans. All of Waco was in an uproar.

Over the years, the trick became known as "Mr. Fouts' strip act."

Sometimes simple tricks can be funny, but not all tricks are very nice and not all tricks are fun. Those that hurt other people or hurt their feelings are not nice tricks to play.

Some people will try to trick you by leading you away from God's word or Jesus. You have to be careful. They may try to trick you by telling you that what Jesus said isn't really true, that he isn't really the Son of God.

It's a funny thing about Jesus. His good news does sound too good to be true: Believe in him and you are saved and will go to Heaven one day. But it's true. It's no trick.

Think about a trick somebody played on you. How did it make you feel?

PROVE IT!

Read Matthew 3:1-6, 13-17.

John told Jesus, "I need to be baptized by you. So why do you come for me to baptize you?"

Baylor had a lot to prove in its 2012 season opener. Consider it proven.

The football team had seventeen wins and two bowl games over the past two seasons. A big shadow lay across the program, though: Robert Griffin III was gone to the pros. The Bears had to prove they could win without him.

Thus, head coach Art Briles called the season opener against SMU "a big, big game for us." A win would help the team believe in itself; a loss would be a real setback.

So the Bears proved they were not just a program that rode RGIII's back to success. They went out and buried SMU 59-24.

Senior quarterback Nick Florence proved he

could lead the Bears by throwing four touchdowns. Baylor led 45-10 before he went to the bench, his day's work done.

Briles said his team wanted to prove itself. And, he added, "We did that." Proving itself all year, the team went on to win eight games.

You know how Baylor felt, don't you? You have to prove yourself over and over again. Every time you take a test, you have to prove you're good enough. Every time you play a sport, you have to prove you're good enough.

But here's something scary: Because you're human and make mistakes, you can never be good enough to measure up to God. Even John the Baptist knew he wasn't good enough, and he was God's prophet and Jesus' cousin.

Here's the way it is. You aren't good enough to get to Heaven without Jesus. But you are definitely good enough with him. With Jesus, you have nothing to prove to God.

List some things you have to prove you are good at. Answer this: How can you prove you're good enough to God?

LIVE ACTION

Read James 2:14-17.

Faith without action is dead.

The Florida Gators talked a good game. The Baylor Lady Bears played one.

The 35-0 and top-ranked Lady Bears took on the Gators on March 20, 2012, in the second round of the NCAA Tournament. Some of the Gators started talking before the game, saying they should be favored.

One Gator guard said she didn't see "anything spectacular" in Baylor's 81-40 win in the first round. The Florida center said that she wasn't worried about playing against Baylor's players. She had played overseas ball, and that made her ready. Another Gator barked, "I think it's time to start talking about Florida," about what they'd done and would do.

Once the game began, the talking was over. So was Florida's season. Baylor won in a cakewalk 76-57.

The Gators did have something nice to say after the game. During the on-court handshakes, they graciously urged the Lady Bears to "go win it all."

Of course, that's exactly what they did.

Talk is cheap. By itself, it just isn't worth too much. How much fun is it to sit around and listen to somebody talk? You get all squirmy because you want to get up and do something.

It's that way in your faith life. In church, you may like singing songs and watching baptisms. But sitting through a sermon sometimes is hard, isn't it?

Even Jesus didn't just talk. He almost never was still. He constantly moved from one place to another, healing and teaching.

Just talking about your faith doesn't really show it. You show that Jesus is alive by making your faith alive. You act. You help people and are kind to them — just like Jesus.

List some things you can do tomorrow to show that your faith is alive. Do them.

WEATHERPROOFED

Read Nahum 1:3-5.

God alone controls the wind and the storms.

How about this? Baylor head coach Grant Teaff once used the weather to pull off a stunt that helped his team win a game.

In August 1985, a heat wave hit Central Texas with temperatures reaching 110 degrees. The Bears' first game was against Wyoming, which wasn't used to such heat. Teaff decided he'd psych the Cowboys out.

The local newspaper and TV folks gathered at the stadium one afternoon. Teaff came out "wearing a chef's hat with a skillet in one hand and an egg in the other." He said, "Everyone said it's hot enough to fry an egg inside this stadium; let's see."

He knelt down by the skillet, cracked the egg, and dropped it into the pan. Right away, the egg began to sizzle as cameras flashed.

The picture of Teaff frying that egg went all over the country, including Wyoming. The Bears blasted the Cowboys 39-18. A Wyoming coach confessed that when his players saw the picture of that egg, the game was over.

Teaff later admitted he had preheated the skillet. "It was hot, but not that hot," he said.

You can look out a window and see a storm coming, but you can't stop it, can you? You can do a lot of things, but only God controls the weather.

God has so much power you can't imagine it. But you also can't imagine how much God loves you. He loves you so much that as Jesus he died in pain on a nasty cross for you.

God is so powerful that he can make it rain and can push the clouds around. The weather does what he tells it to. But the strongest thing of all about God is his love for you.

List all the kinds of bad weather you can think of. Tell a parent what you'd do in case of each one.

BEAR FACTS

Read Psalm 139:1-6, 13-14.

I praise God because of the wonderful way you made me.

Some Texas A&M students once hurt their own team. They kidnapped the Baylor bears.

The Aggies were favored in the 1950 game, but the Baylor fans and players were really fired up. That's because sometime during the week several A&M cadets had made off with Baylor's two bear cub mascots.

A&M took a quick 13-0 lead in the game, but after that the day belonged to Baylor and quarterback Larry Isbell. He was such a good athlete that he was All-America in both football (1951) and baseball (1952).

Isbell threw four touchdown passes against A&M that day. He also punted the ball. Baylor came from behind to win 27-20.

By then, the stolen bear cubs had been returned to their Waco home. The bearnappers wanted nothing to do with them anymore.

How come? Stuck in a car with nothing to do, the critters had had a whole lot of fun. With their claws and their teeth, they ripped the car's back seat to shreds.

We respect and admire animals such as bears. Isn't it fun on a trip to spot wild turkeys, foxes, or deer in the woods? And a zoo is one of the most fun places in the world to visit. Who in the world could dream up a walrus, a moose, a prairie dog, or a bear?

Well, God thought them all up, just like he did the armadillo and the horse. And just like he thought you up.

You are special. You are one of a kind, the only person in the world God made like you. If you wore a label like the one you have on your shirts, it might say: "Lovingly handmade in Heaven by #1 — God."

How special does it make you feel to know that God himself made you? Share that feeling with your parents.

THE BAD TIMES

Read Luke 18:7-8.

God will make things right one day for those who follow Jesus.

Baylor fans still remember the worst thing ever to happen to the school even though it happened a long time ago.

In January 1927, the Baylor basketball team traveled by bus to Austin for a game against Texas. It was raining. In Round Rock, the bus neared a railroad crossing. Buildings hid a speeding passenger train. The engineer blew the whistle, but no one on the bus heard it.

Head coach Ralph Wolf was the first one to see the train. He told the driver, who acted quickly. He just didn't have enough time. The train struck the rear of the bus. Ten of the twenty-one players, coaches, and fans on the bus were killed.

"Abe" Kelly, who was also a football captain,

pushed a teammate out of the window before the collision. It saved his life, but Kelly was one of the ten who died.

Each year, Baylor freshmen hear the story of The Immortal Ten, as they are known. They take part in a candlelight ceremony. In 2007, a memorial to the Ten was erected on campus.

Grown-ups sometimes think kids don't have any problems. But children, like adults, have some bad times. Some of them don't just go away overnight, do they? Like getting sick. Or having a friend turn on you and make fun of you. Or having someone you love die.

Life is hard, even if you're a Christian. Faith in Jesus Christ doesn't give you a pass on life's bad times. But faith in Jesus does give you help and strength in getting through them.

You keep the faith. You pray. You trust. You know that someday God will make it right for you. The bad times are not forever; your faith should be.

Recall a time things were bad for you. Thank God for helping you get through it.

NERVOUS NELLIE

Read Mark 5:1-13.

The demon begged, "Jesus, promise you won't hurt me!"

A Baylor star was nervous about meeting the King of England. That didn't keep him from straightening the king out about Texas.

In 1948, Jackie Robinson (not the one from baseball) became Baylor's third All-American basketball player. He was then named to the 1948 U.S. Olympic Team. The Americans won the gold medal in London.

Robinson represented the U.S. team at a tea with the royal family at Buckingham Palace. He said he was "awfully nervous" when he shook King George VI's hand. "He couldn't have been nicer," Robinson said.

Later, Robinson and some other athletes, including a swimmer from California, were talking with the king. He exclaimed, "California!

Bears

That's where the biggest and best come from!" Nervous no longer, Robinson spoke up to tell the king that the biggest and best came from Texas, not California.

Like Baylor's Jackie Robinson, you get nervous sometimes. Before a big test maybe. Or before a big game. How about having to make a speech? Whoowee, that's tough.

Have you ever thought that you make other people nervous? That there's one for sure who really gets nervous about you? Who in the world? Believe it or not, it's Satan himself. Yep, that's the one.

As a Christian, you make Satan nervous because you stand before him with the power of Jesus Christ to use. When you live for Jesus, you spend the day making the devil himself downright miserable.

So go out there and have a good time making Satan nervous. Do everything in Jesus' name.

At a mirror, say the name of Jesus out loud and act out how a nervous, scared devil might react.

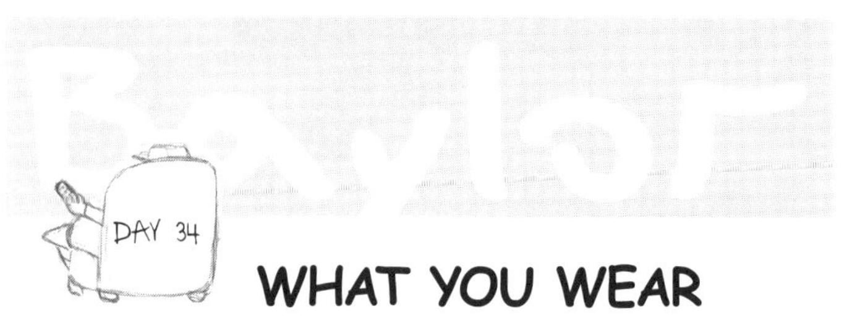

WHAT YOU WEAR

Read Genesis 37:1-5.

His father made Joseph a pretty coat, and his brothers hated him.

The truth came out in New York City. Robert Griffin III won the Heisman Trophy in part because of his socks.

On Saturday, Dec. 11, 2011, Baylor's junior quarterback won the Heisman Trophy as the nation's best college football player. Baylor head coach Art Briles said RGIII won the prize because of his "dedication and discipline."

Griffin showed there may have been something else that helped him. He was dressed in a black pinstripe suit at the presentation ceremony. While there, he lifted a pants leg to uncover a pair of Superman socks.

It turned out they were just one pair in the quarterback's collection of goofy socks. A lot of them featured cartoon characters. During

Beats

an interview with *ESPN*, he showed off a pair of Elmo socks. At various times, he wore the Cookie Monster, Angry Birds, and SpongeBob SquarePants.

Heisman Trophy night, though, required a dash of Superman.

You dress a certain way for school and for church. How silly would it be to wear shoes and a coat into a swimming pool?

Your clothes wear out and you outgrow them. So you change clothes all the time. Getting a new pair of shoes or some new jeans changes the way you look. It doesn't change you, does it? You're still the same person.

Do you think Jesus cares about the clothes you wear? What he cares about is your heart. What he cares about is how you act. It doesn't matter whether you're wearing clothes fit for a king or rags a homeless person might wear.

Clothes don't make you the person you are. Loving Jesus does.

Dress up in a wild outfit. Before a mirror, act out what Jesus would say to you if he saw you.

BIG MISTAKE

Read Mark 14:66-72.

Peter remembered Jesus had said to him, "Three times you will say you don't know me." Peter cried.

To save their season, all the Bears had to do was get the ball in bounds. And they blew it.

The Baylor men's basketball team of 2013-14 needed to beat Oklahoma State to keep their NCAA Tournament hopes alive. They had the game all wrapped up — or so they thought.

They led 58-55 with only 3.5 seconds left in the game. And the Bears had the ball. They just had to get the ball in bounds for the win.

To the horror of Baylor fans, the Cowboys stole the inbounds pass and nailed a 3-point shot at the buzzer. Thanks to a big old mistake, the game went into overtime.

The Bears recovered from their big blunder. Senior Corey Jefferson hit a three to start the

OT, and the Bears went on to win 70-64.

The team got hot, won seven of its last eight games, and landed in the Big Dance.

Only one person has ever walked this Earth and been perfect. That was Jesus. You're not him. That means you will make mistakes. You will not make all hundreds on your tests. You will not make every play in softball or soccer. You will trip and fall sometimes and embarrass yourself. You will be mean to others sometime.

All your mistakes can be forgiven if you ask God for forgiveness. That means God forgets about them. Even Peter's awful mistake in denying that he knew Jesus was forgiven because he came back to Jesus. He went on to be the one of the greatest men in the history of the Church.

The one mistake you must never make is to kick Jesus out of your life completely. God won't forget about that one.

What mistakes did you make today that hurt other people? Ask God for forgiveness of them.

I TOLD YOU SO

Read Matthew 24:30-35.

Jesus will come on the clouds in power and glory.

Billy Patterson could have told Texas "I told you so." Instead, some Baylor fans from his hometown did it for him.

A quarterback nicknamed "Bullet" Bill, Patterson was the Southwest Conference MVP in 1937 and a second-team All-America in 1938.

He was an outstanding high school player in Hillsboro. Some local folks wanted him to play for Texas. They set up a meeting between Bullet Bill and the Longhorn head coach at the Andrews Cafe in Hillsboro. Patterson showed up but the Texas coach never came.

So he wound up at Baylor. As a sophomore against Texas, he led the Bears to three touchdowns in the fourth quarter and a 21-18 win. After the game, he could have said "I told you so" to the Texas coaches. He didn't need to.

A whole bunch of Hillsboro folks at the game went up to the Texas head coach. They made sure he knew the kid who beat him was the one he had stood up in Hillsboro.

One day Jesus is going to come back and find everyone who has been faithful to him. He will gather them all up and take them to Heaven. There they will live with God forever in happiness and love. It will be the most glorious time of all.

How do we know that's going to happen? Jesus told us so. When will it happen? Well, he didn't tell us that. He just told us to be ready so we don't miss it.

How do you get ready? It's simple. You just love Jesus. You live your life for Jesus. You remember that Jesus is counting on you, and you do everything for him.

Are you ready?

Put some ice cream in a bowl and watch it melt to remind you that Jesus may come back at any time, maybe even before the ice cream melts.

MAMA SAID

Read John 19:25-27.

Jesus' mother, Mary, stood near his cross.

Kim Mulkey wanted to chew her team out at halftime of a basketball game. She couldn't because she had to be a mom.

Baylor's Hall-of-Fame head coach watched Texas nail a three to take a one-point lead at halftime. Tonight, though, she would not be going to the locker room to talk to her players.

It was Family Night 2014, a night when the players and their families took the court at halftime together. So Mulkey stood at center court with her starting senior forward. She was her daughter, Makenzie Robertson.

One unwritten rule of college sports is that a player never picks a school because of a coach. This time the rule was broken. Robertson didn't even think about the offers she received. Her dream was to play college ball for her mom.

They made it work, separating coach from mother. "Anything she says to me on the court," I never take personally," Robertson said. "It's two different roles: mom and coach."

Mulkey had one regret about her daughter. She didn't want to show favors, and so she didn't play her enough until her senior year.

By the way, the Bears whipped Texas 87-73.

Mamas do a lot for their kids, and they do it all out of love. Even when your mama tells you to do something you don't want to, she has a good reason. It's usually for your good.

Think about Jesus' mama for a minute. She loved her boy no matter what. When Mary stood near the cross, she was showing both love and courage. No matter how wrong it was, Jesus was condemned as an enemy of the Roman Empire. She could have been, too.

Love your mama like she loves you.

Make a list of the things your mama did for you today. Did you thank her? Do you thank God for her?

HOLLYWOOD ENDING

Read Luke 24:1-8.

Jesus is not here! He has risen!

No way Hollywood would make a movie out of Grant Teaff's last game at Baylor. Nobody would believe it.

In August, the winningest football coach in Baylor history announced that the '92 season would be his last. His final game was against Texas, which was favored.

Knee surgery had sidelined senior defensive back Trooper Taylor for the whole season. But he told Teaff, "I want to play in your last game and my last game." Teaff refused.

During the game, Taylor kept asking his coach to put him in. Teaff finally gave in and sent him in for one play late in the game.

Baylor led 21-20, but Texas was at the Bear 39 with two minutes left. They needed two yards for the first down. "Out of nowhere," a defender stopped the Texas back inches short of the first down. Baylor then ran out the clock.

And who was it who made that tackle and gave a happy ending to Teaff's last game? It was Trooper Taylor!

Movies are fun, aren't they? Sitting in the dark with your family or friends watching all the action on a big screen. Chomping on popcorn or chewing on Milk Duds or Junior Mints. That is really cool. Life is good.

Movies often have happy endings. Lots of folks will tell you that happy endings are just for the movies. Or fairy tales. That life always winds up with sadness. But that's another of the world's lies.

Jesus has been coming up with happy endings for two thousand years. When you trust in Jesus, your life will have a happy ending. One too good even for Hollywood.

With faith in Jesus, you live with God and Jesus in peace, joy, and love. Forever. The End.

List your five favorite movies.
Tell why you like them.
Do they have happy endings?

THE JESUS WAY

Read Romans 13:10-12.

Behave decently like in the daytime, the way Jesus would.

Mickey Sullivan had a way of coaching that was all his own. It worked.

Sullivan took over as head coach of Baylor's baseball team in 1974. He coached for 21 seasons and won 649 games. His 1977 and 1978 teams made it to the College World Series.

What was the Sullivan way? "We were a bit looser," explained pitcher Jonathan Perlman, who made it to the major leagues.

For instance, Sullivan wasn't too much for giving fancy signs from his third-base coaching box. "If you were on first base, he might tilt his head toward second," said Marty Crawford, a star second baseman. That meant Sullivan wanted the runner to steal.

He was a player's coach who loved walk-ons.

He always let his hitters swing away.

After Sullivan won his 600th game, his team presented him a pipe as a present. In a later game, he puffed away in the dugout. Suddenly, he lost his temper at a bad play and threw the pipe.

It bounced off the floor, hit a wall, and then bounced back to Sullivan. He caught it and calmly kept on puffing. The dugout went nuts.

Even as a young person, you have a certain way that you live. You're a Baylor fan. Maybe you live in the country. Or in town. Do you wear jeans to school? Or shorts? You have a favorite video game and TV show.

Then there's your faith. You're a Christian. That means that as a way of life, you follow Jesus. You do your best to act and to think like Jesus would. That means you always try to act in a loving manner toward other people.

It's The Jesus Way. It should be your way.

Make up a story about Jesus being at your school. Tell how you think he would act in class and in the lunchroom.

LET'S EAT!

Read Genesis 9:1-3.

I now give you everything that lives and moves to eat.

Grant Teaff did about anything he could to help his team get ready for Texas. He even ate a worm.

Before the 1978 game, the Baylor head coach told the story of two ice fishermen. They were only a few feet apart. One caught fish, the other didn't. The unsuccessful fisherman asked the other man his secret. He put a worm in his mouth and said, "You've got to keep the worms warm."

On Saturday before the Bears took the field, Teaff gave a pep talk. He ended by saying he could help his team win by keeping the worms warm. He then held a worm up and dropped it into his mouth.

The fired-up Bears tore onto the field while

the head coach "popped [his] little friend into the trash."

One of the assistant coaches told him, "I'm glad you didn't call for volunteers."

The Bears ate Texas up 38-14.

Americans really do love food. We love to eat all sorts of different things, from hamburgers to chicken, pizza to ice cream — just maybe not worms. We even have TV channels that talk about food all the time. They show people how to make new dishes for their family to try and eat.

Food is one of God's really good ideas. Isn't it amazing to think that from one apple seed, an entire tree full of apples can grow and give you apples year after year?

God created this system that lets all living things grow and nourish one another. Your food comes from God and nowhere else. The least you can do is thank him for it.

Three questions to answer: What's your favorite food? What can you cook? Do you always thank God before you eat?

NAME DROPPING

Read Exodus 3:13-15.

Moses asked God what his name was. God answered, "Tell them I AM *has sent you."*

From the Stork to the White Freak, the 2013 Baylor football team had a lot of nicknames.

Head coach Art Briles stamped a nickname on just about every player he had. Kicker Aaron Jones was dubbed "Stork." Jones liked it so much he even used the Twitter nickname "StorkTheDork."

Backup quarterback Andrew Frerking got hit with "White Freak." Tevin Reese, who set the NCAA record for career touchdown receptions longer than 40 yards, was "Sweet Feet."

One of the players has come to be known more by his nickname than his given name. He is running back Shock Linwood, who rushed for 1251 yards as a sophomore in 2014. His real

Bears

name is Rashodrick Antoine Linwood. He was born during a time when Shaquille O'Neal's "Shaq Attack" nickname was the big thing. His mom decided that he would be the "Shock Attack." It got shortened to just "Shock."

Nicknames are not given to people or to athletes any old way. They are often fun or funny names that say something about who that person is, on or off the field. First names can do the same thing; they can say a lot about a person to other people.

In the Bible, people's names reflect who they are, too. Biblical names show us a little something about that person's personality or how he or she acts.

The same works with God's name. To know the name of God is to know how he has shown himself to us.

As for you, what do you think your name says about you to God? Remember this: Just as you know God's name, he knows yours, too.

Have an adult help you look up the meaning of your first name. Does it match who you are and what you're like?

POP THE QUESTION

Read Matthew 16:13-17.

Jesus asked his disciples, "Who do you think I am?"

The broadcasters all said Baylor had to answer a question to beat Creighton. They had the wrong question.

In March 2014, the Bears played the Creighton Bluejays in the NCAA men's basketball tournament. The birds had one of the greatest scorers in college basketball history. So everybody asked the question: Could Baylor even slow him down?

Wrong question. Wrong team. They should have asked Creighton a question: Could the Jays handle the really good team Baylor had become? The answer was "NO!"

The game was a blow-out. The Bears beat Creighton 85-55 to advance to the Sweet 16 in the tournament. The game was tied at 7-7 when Baylor went on a 12-0 run. With most of the first half still to go, the game was over.

That great scorer? He scored only three points in the first half and didn't hit a single field goal until Baylor was ahead 35-16.

In school, others have questions for you. Outside school, you have questions for others. Hey, what's for supper? Can I go outside and play? When are we going on vacation? What kind of team will Baylor have this year?

Some questions aren't really a big deal. One question, though, is the most important one you will ever ask and answer. It's the one that Jesus asked Peter: "Who do you say I am?" Peter gave the one and only correct answer: "Jesus, you are the Son of God."

Why is that question so important that it is the only one that matters? The answer decides how you spend your life — walking with Jesus — and how you spend all of eternity — living with Jesus.

Tell your parents in your words the answer to this question: Who is Jesus?

YOU CAN'T DO THAT!

Read Matthew 19:23-26.

With God all things are possible.

They all said Eddie Lackey was too small and too slow to play big-time college football. He didn't pay a lick of attention to them.

Lackey couldn't find any college coach who would take him on his team after high school. He was only 5-11, 200 lbs., and didn't have blazing speed. Too small, too slow, they said.

So he went to smaller colleges for two seasons and played well. He still believed he could play big-time ball, though.

In Waco, Baylor's defensive coaches looked over some tapes hoping to find a player. They spotted Lackey and invited him to a game. He said he'd be glad to show up since he had nowhere else to go. He was so excited that he committed to Baylor before he left campus.

So he was too small and too slow, right?

The second Baylor game Lackey ever saw he started. This player who wouldn't let others tell him what he couldn't do was an All-Big 12 linebacker in both 2012 and 2013.

Has anybody ever told you that you couldn't do something because you weren't big enough or smart enough or good enough? You can't make straight A's; you can't play soccer; you can't sing or dance in front of everybody.

Maybe it's time you ignored what everybody says. Maybe it's time that you listened to God instead.

Most people see you as you are. God does, too, but God also sees you as you can be. In God's eyes, you can do just about anything — if you depend upon God. That means you let God guide you and lead you. You do God's will.

Yes, you can do it if God wants you to. You pray like everything depends on God and work like everything depends on you.

Think of something you'd like to do but somebody said you weren't good enough. Start praying about it and working on it.

KEEPING THE PEACE

Read Hebrews 12:14-15.

Do all you can to live in peace with everyone.

Baylor and Texas A&M stopped playing each other in all sports for a while in 1926. That's because at the football game, a riot broke out that left one A&M student dead.

At halftime, some Baylor students drove a truck onto the field. They carried signs that had scores of recent Bear wins over A&M. But what really got the Aggie students upset was that the Baylor guys were wearing women's clothes. Calling them sissies was just too big of an insult for the Aggies to take.

Some A&M students charged the truck, and they weren't smiling about it. A big fight broke out. It stopped only when the A&M band started playing the national anthem. As good military guys do, the cadets snapped to attention. One Aggie, though, was taken to a hospital with a head injury and died there.

The Aggies went home and loaded a cannon onto a railroad car. They were headed back to Waco. Some Texas Rangers stepped in and put a stop to it before it all got worse.

It's a good thing that students today don't usually get into fights at games. But have you ever played in a game of some kind where a player from the other team hurt you? Maybe you wanted to fight because of it.

No matter what happens, no matter where you are, no matter what someone else has done to you — fighting is never the answer. It's not just because you make an enemy. It's also because Jesus said you should make peace and make a friend instead of fighting.

Making peace often isn't as easy as taking a swing or saying ugly things to someone. It does requires more courage. It's also exactly what Jesus would do.

Try talking to a person at school you don't get along with and making him or her your friend.

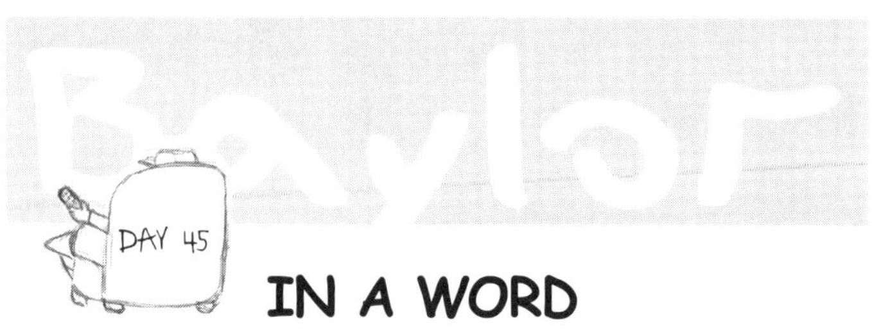

IN A WORD

Read Matthew 12:33-37.

A good man says good things, but an evil man speaks evil words.

Kim Mulkey had thirty seconds to say something that would save Baylor's national title hopes. She said it.

In 2005, the 31-3 Lady Bears met LSU in the Final Four semifinals. Baylor was in real trouble in the first half. LSU led 24-9. "We're getting embarrassed on national television," Mulkey, the Baylor coach, said. She was right.

She called a time out. Just what could she say? Maybe that no one in the history of the women's Final Four had ever come back from a 15-point deficit and won? Probably not that.

Mulkey first said nothing. She simply smiled. Then she said three things: 1) relax; 2) remember they had come back against LSU earlier that year; 3) switch to a zone defense.

Bears

The players listened and found their groove again. They went on a 19-4 run that tied the game at halftime. LSU never recovered; Baylor won 68-57.

They then blew Michigan State out 84-62. They were national champs, their run kept alive by a few words from their head coach.

Words can hurt. When somebody at school says ugly things to you or calls you a name, it hurts your feelings, doesn't it?

Words have power for good or for bad. The words you speak at school or on the ballfield can make other kids cry. But they can also make your friends feel good and smile.

Don't ever make the mistake of thinking what you say doesn't matter. Speaking the Word of God was the only way Jesus had of getting his message to others. Look what he managed to do.

Watch what you say; others sure will.

With a parent, listen to three songs on the radio. Decide if what they say is good or bad. Promise you will listen only to music with good words.

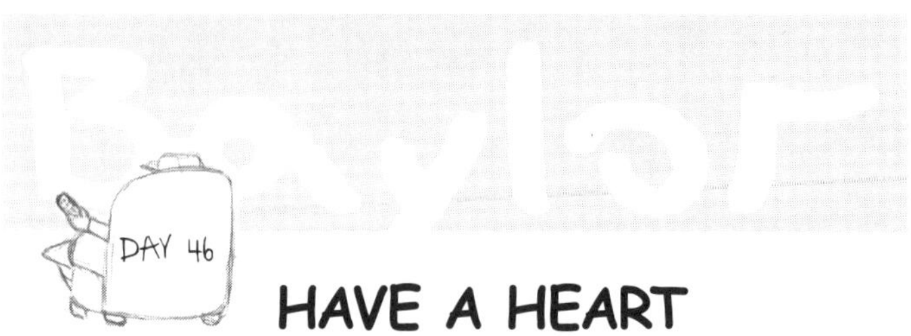

HAVE A HEART

Matthew 6:19-24.

You can't serve two masters. You will love one and hate the other.

Following the 2009 season, Baylor head football coach Art Briles had a decision to make. He went with his heart and stayed at Baylor.

Being the head football coach at Texas Tech may well have been Briles "dream job" at one time. After all, he graduated from Texas Tech, and so did his wife. He had grown up in West Texas as a fan of the Red Raiders.

When the job came open, the Tech officials looked toward Waco and Baylor's head coach. Remember, this was after Briles' first two seasons. Both of those teams went 4-8 and nobody was really happy. Including Briles.

Briles was told by some Tech people that he could have the job if he wanted it. The boss bear said he spent four nights tossing and turning as he tried to decide.

Taking the Tech job made sense. At the time, he didn't know if the fan support at Baylor would ever fill the stadium. It looked as though he could win more games at Tech.

In the end, though, he wasn't ready to give up on Baylor or his quarterback, Robert Griffin III. Art Briles went with his heart. It turned out to be a very good choice.

Sometimes you must make a choice. Some other boys or girls might want you to do something that you know in your heart isn't right. Like cheat on a test or lie to your parents.

Your head says be cool and go along with the crowd. Your heart says it's wrong. How do you decide? Flip a coin? Use a dart board?

Nah. You turn to the one who should be number one in your life: Jesus. You figure out what Jesus would do.

Your head tells you what Jesus wants you to do. Your heart tells you that it is right to do it.

Pretend somebody wants to give you an answer to a test question. Make up an answer Jesus would give you about it.

THE INTERVIEW

Read Romans 14:9-12.

We will all have to explain to God everything we have done.

Receiver Kendall Wright worked real hard to improve his pass catching. He needed some work, too, on his interviews.

At an interview, people — especially news reporters — ask a person questions. When reporters first tried to interview Wright at Baylor in 2008, he didn't say too much.

All-American tackle Jason Smith saw a reporter trying to interview Smith. He shook his head, walked over, and said to Wright, "Man you've got to give him more than that." That is, Wright had to talk more.

Smith told the reporter to ask him a question, and he would pretend to be the receiver. So the reporter asked, "What have you been working on to get better?" Without cracking a smile, Smith answered, "Catching."

Wright got the message and worked to get better with his interviews. He even took a class. He had to improve because he became an All-American pass catcher who tied or set sixteen records. That meant he did a lot of interviews.

When grown-ups get famous (like Kendall Wright) or want a job, they have an interview. They answer questions from people.

You'll probably have a job interview one day. Sooner than that, you may have an interview at a pageant or to get into a school club.

Interviews are hard because people ask you questions and judge you. That means they decide whether you are good enough for what they want. Nobody likes to be judged.

One day, you will show up in Heaven. The Bible tells us that we all will be judged by God. You will have an interview with God.

Talk about being nervous! How in the world can you be good enough for God? All it takes is Jesus. Jesus makes you good enough.

Pretend you're being interviewed by God. What would you tell him about yourself?

ALL TIRED OUT

Read Matthew 11:27-30.

Jesus said, "Come to me and I will give you rest."

Baylor's offense scored so fast and so much that kicker Aaron Jones sometimes got tired.

Jones is the greatest placekicker in Baylor history and one of college football's best ever. Helped out by Baylor's point-a-minute-offense, he set a bunch of records. He kicked the most extra points in college history.

In high school, he was a soccer player but didn't get any college offers. So he walked on the Baylor football team in 2009. He didn't get into any games that season.

In 2010, head coach Art Briles held an open competition at practice to find the kicker for his football team. Jones won the job.

He was so active that kicking sometimes tired him out. After all, he kicked all the field goals and PATs and the kickoffs. That meant he had to run down the field to cover. He also spent most of every game warming up on the sideline by kicking into a net.

In the 66-42 stomping of Texas Tech in 2011, he kicked off eleven times and booted nine extra points and a field goal. "That's the most tired I've ever been," he said.

Don't you just get tired sometime? Maybe after a tough day at school when you stayed up too late the night before. Have you ever gotten so tired on a trip that you fell asleep in the back seat of the car?

Everybody gets tired, especially grown-ups. And sometimes, like grown-ups, you have to do what Aaron Jones had to do. You have to keep going no matter how tired you are.

That's a good time to pray to Jesus. When you do that, you have the power of almighty God to help you and give you strength.

Talk about the last time you fell asleep on the floor. Why were you so tired? Did you know God can give you strength?

HOW EMBARRASSING!

Read John 2:1-11.

Jesus' mother told him they had run out of wine at the wedding.

The Bears were about to pull off a collapse that would embarrass the whole team. Then their All-American catcher saved the day — and the game.

On their way to the 2011 NCAA Tournament, the Baylor baseball team simply slaughtered Texas Tech on March 19. For eight innings.

It was a wacky game all the way. Three times, Baylor scored four runs on only one hit. One player walked and then scored on two errors.

As the ninth inning started, Baylor led 13-4. Then the wacky game got downright crazy.

Incredibly, Texas Tech scored nine runs. Six of them came after two outs. When Baylor at last got the third out, the score — embarrassingly — was tied at 13.

Bears

The embarrassment continued when the first two Bears made outs in the bottom of the ninth. But a hit batsman and a single sent catcher Josh Ludy to the plate. He delivered a single to drive home a run. The Bears had managed to avoid an embarrassing defeat.

Ever been to a birthday party where they ran out of pizza or soda? Ever said something really dumb or tripped over your own feet right in front of everybody? Man, that's embarrassing! We've all been there, done that.

Embarrassment helps sometimes because it teaches us not to do that again. Too many of us, though, are embarrassed by our faith. We won't claim the name of Jesus in public.

But here's the awful flip side. If you're embarrassed by Jesus, then he's embarrassed by you. That means that when you appear before God one day, Jesus won't know who you are so he can save you and lead you into Heaven.

That's not embarrassing. That's horrible.

Is there anything about Jesus that embarrasses you? Why? Come up with ways to get rid of it.

BEING DIFFERENT

Read Daniel 3:14-29.

"King, we won't serve your gods or worship your gold statue."

Grant Teaff was searching for a way to put some pride back into Baylor football. He found it in "The Difference at Baylor."

The Bears had won only three games in the last three seasons when Teaff took over in 1972. He needed to change the attitude, to put some pride in the players and the fans.

Some students helped him out. Before the A&M game, they came to the coach's office. One said that because he was a Christian coach at a Christian school, they wanted to hand out a pamphlet at the game. It was called "The Difference at Baylor." Inside it was a quote from the coach: "The greatest victory is not on the football field but through a personal relationship with Jesus Christ." Teaff approved the idea.

One assistant said it looked like they were saying winning was not important. "We'll win," Teaff said. He was right. The Bears won 15-13.

If you're a Christian, then you're different just like Baylor is different from other places because it's a Christian school. You see, the world wants you to act in a certain way while Jesus wants you to act another, different way.

Jesus wants you to worship and be true to God and his Word. Those who don't believe in God or Jesus may make fun of you for living that way. You have to decide. Do you stay with Jesus or do you turn your back on him?

You are different but it's the most wonderful difference of all. As a Christian, you are a child of God. God knows you by name just as your parents do.

The world doesn't like for you to be different. Jesus praises and loves you for it.

With your parents, watch a TV show with a family on it. Find ways they act and talk differently from your family.

ONE-MAN ARMY

Read Revelation 19:11-16.

The armies of heaven were following him on white horses.

One time, a Baylor football player said he'd play the other team by himself.

Before the 1910 game, the Baylor and Texas coaches disagreed about the refs. Texas won out and picked an official who had close ties to the school.

As the game wore on, the suspect ref "was giving Texas all the better of it in his calls." He even got in front of a Baylor player one time to slow him down so Texas could catch up and tackle him.

Baylor finally had enough. After still another bad call, the Baylor coach led his players off the field, ending the game.

Except for one. E.T. "Bull" Adams, "a mighty linebacker" who was also a great student, refused to go. He said he would act as a one-man army. He challenged Texas to run plays between the tackles. If they would, he said, he'd take them on all by himself.

Texas declined the offer and took the 1-0 win. Baylor insisted it was a 6-6 tie.

Do you picture Jesus as a gentle man who heals sick people and loves children?

That's how he was the first time around. But the Bible tells us Jesus will come back one day and he will look and act a whole lot different. He will be a warrior and will lead an army.

What will Jesus do at the head of his army? He will destroy all the bad people in this world, those who hurt others, who don't believe in him, and who curse the name of God.

It sounds scary and it is — but not if you believe Jesus is God's son and the Lord of all.

Think about this. For now — and until Jesus comes back — you're a soldier in Jesus' army. You can help conquer the world for Jesus.

Read Revelation 19:11-16 again. Then draw a picture of how Jesus looks as the Bible says he does.

GIVING UP

Read Numbers 13:25-28, 30-32.

Some men said, "We can't attack those people because they are bigger and stronger than we are."

Players quit football all the time. How many, though, almost quit because of the weather?

Cyril Richardson was an All-American guard at Baylor in 2013. But he almost didn't even play high-school ball.

He was a freshman in high school in New Orleans when Hurricane Katrina hit. His family had to flee for their lives. He spent the next two years moving from place to place.

The moves wrecked his football career and left him behind in school. He lost his whole sophomore year, and that's when Richardson decided to quit football. Fortunately, his brother talked him out of it. He finally made it onto a field his junior year of high school.

Bears

But his grades were a mess. That turned out to be good news for Baylor. Because he was in summer school, he missed a TCU football camp. He had caught up on his work, though, by the time Baylor had a camp, so he went.

At the end of the day, the player who almost quit because of the weather, got a scholarship.

Everybody feels like quitting at some time or another. Maybe football is harder than you thought it was. Maybe you just can't figure out math no matter how much you study. Maybe you and a friend just don't get along anymore.

Quitting is easy. But when it comes to God, remember the story of the people of Israel. They quit when the Promised Land was theirs for the taking. They forgot that God would never, ever give up on them.

God never quits on you either. So you must never give up on God even if it seems like your prayers aren't getting through. You just don't know what God may be up to. The only way to find out is to never quit on God.

Winners never quit; quitters never win. How does this apply to God and you?

HOW DISAPPOINTING!

Read Ezra 3:10-12.

Many older priests sobbed out loud.
They had seen the first temple.
Others shouted for joy.

For Raynor Campbell, 2009 was the most disappointing year of his young life. But he would never take it back.

Campbell began playing baseball when he was 6 years old in Norway, of all places. He chose Baylor because "it felt like home" with its Christian environment.

He was a freshman All-America in 2007 and the big 12 Freshman of the Year. He hit .311 in 2008 despite a thumb injury.

Then came 2009. The hits just quit coming and playing shortstop got tougher. He was dropped to the bottom of the lineup. "It was very frustrating," Campbell said.

So why wouldn't he do away with that awful,

disappointing season if he could? "It taught me so much," he said. "I became a better Christian and . . . a better ballplayer."

He enjoyed a "righteous rebirth" in 2010. He hit .335, was second-team All-Big 12, and was drafted by the San Francisco Giants.

Like grown-ups, you've been disappointed, haven't you? It happens when you expect something and don't get it. Or someone you know acts in a way you didn't expect them to.

The truth is that your parents, your grandparents, your friends at school, your teachers, your sisters and/or brothers — they will all disappoint you at some time. But don't be too mad at them. You will disappoint all of them sometime, too. It's part of being human.

When you are disappointed, remember as Raynor Campbell did to keep your eyes on God. Your life may be disappointing at the moment, but God is still good to you.

God never disappoints.

Read Ezra 3:10-12 again.
Why were some priests crying?
How do you think God felt about that?

FAMILY MAN

Read Mark 3:31-35.

Jesus said, "Whoever does God's will is my family."

Baylor legend Lawrence Elkins helped shape the future of college football after he had been shaped by his family.

Elkins was All-America at Baylor in 1964. No one had ever seen anything like quarterback Don Trull throwing to Elkins. He set a national record with 70 catches in 1963.

Elkins was great because he worked hard. Growing up, he had to. His father was gassed in World War I and was disabled. Elkins had nine brothers and sisters, and he went to work early to help put food on the table.

His mother had been married before to the man famous as the Santa Claus bank robber. He had robbed a bank in 1927 while wearing a Santa Claus suit. His gang was caught when their car ran out of gas. He was hanged.

Elkins' older brothers would throw a football at him as hard as they could. "I don't think I quit crying until I was 16," he said.

When he did, at Baylor, this family man let fans see what football's future looked like.

Somebody once said that families are like fudge, mostly sweet with a few nuts. You can probably name your sweet kinfolks — and the nutty ones too.

You may not like it all the time, but you have a family. You can blame God for that. God loves the idea of family so much that he chose to live in one as a son, a brother, and a cousin. Jesus had a family.

But Jesus also had a new definition for what makes up a family. It's not just blood. It's a choice. Everybody who does God's will is a member of Jesus' family.

That includes you. You have family members all over the place who stand ready to love you because you're all part of God's big family.

With help from a parent or grandparent, draw your family tree.

THE GOOD OLD DAYS

Read Psalm 102:1-5.

Lord, my days disappear like smoke.

The "good old days" weren't really very good for women's basketball at Baylor.

What can be called the modern era of Baylor women's basketball began in 1973 with the first scholarship given to a woman. It was basketball legend Suzie Snider.

In those days, they were the Bearettes. They didn't even have tryouts. Sue Turner called the coach and said she wanted to play basketball. The coach told her to show up for practice. She did and she was on the team.

They had money for uniforms and overnight stays. That was all. Turner said the girls drove their own cars to games, paying for their own gas and food. They weren't awarded letters even though they played for Baylor.

Bears

As late as 1979, head coach Pam Bowers washed the girls' jerseys and drove the team bus to games. The games were free since nobody sold tickets. The band didn't play at the women's games, and there was no tip-off club to support the team.

The "good old days" have surely gotten a lot better for women's basketball at Baylor.

Baylor women's basketball isn't like it used to be because time doesn't stand still. That means things change. When they do, you wind up with memories, things you remember. What grade are you in now? Remember some of the things you did last year? Remember your baptism?

You will always have those memories. God is always with you, too. Today may be one of those good old days you will remember someday, but you must share it with God. A true "good old day" is one God is a part of.

Make a list of things you can do to make God a part of your day (like saying a blessing). Try to do them all.

YOUR GOALS

Read 1 Peter 1:7-9.

Because of your faith, you are receiving your goal, which is the salvation of your soul.

Once, the Baylor Bears and their fans went nuts because the football team got to play in a bowl game. Funny how times have changed.

On Oct. 23, 2010, Baylor beat Kansas State for the Bears' sixth win of the season. That meant the team had accomplished one of its goals: win at least six games. That made the Bears eligible for a bowl game.

The win touched off a wild celebration. Fans "stampeded out of the stands [and] partied with the Baylor players." Special edition newspapers were released, spreading the good, big news with the headline "Bowl Bound."

But that was then. With that goal reached, head coach Art Briles and his team set some bigger ones. Now Baylor expected to play in a bowl game. The sights were set on a Big 12 championship and a BCS (a big-time) bowl and even the national championship.

So there was little celebration after Baylor whipped Iowa State 71-7 in 2013. That was the team's sixth win, but it was not a big deal any more. The Bears had come a long way in three seasons; so had their goals.

You have goals in your life. Maybe to get better at soccer, math, or a video game. Or to make all A's in school. Maybe you want to earn a spot in the band or on the track team.

You have goals in your faith life, too. You go to church to worship God. You read the Bible to learn more about God. But what's your goal? What is all that stuff about?

The goal of your faith life is to get to Heaven. If you are saved by believing in Jesus, then someday you will be with Jesus and with God in Heaven.

Make a list of the goals you want to reach in school and in church this year.

A FAITHFUL LIFE

Read Hebrews 11:1-3, 6.

Without faith, you can't please God.

Grant Teaff stepped out on faith. Baylor fans have been forever grateful.

The school was looking for a head football coach in 1971, and it wasn't going well. Baylor didn't have the money to land a big-name coach. Rumor said more than a dozen coaches had turned the job down. The athletic director finally hired the head coach at New Mexico.

Teaff had no interest at all in the job. His plan was to become the head coach at Texas Tech. Thus, he was shocked at what his wife said when she saw the news of the hiring on TV. "You are going to Baylor," she said. Teaff just laughed and said, "Baylor has a coach."

The next day, the coach changed his mind. The athletic director called Teaff, a longtime friend. He still wasn't interested, but the AD convinced him to take a visit and talk it over.

Teaff was impressed by the commitment he saw. "I stepped out on faith alone and [took] the job," he said. Twenty-one seasons later, he retired as Baylor's winningest coach ever.

In your life, you have faith in many things. Faith in people like your parents, your grandparents, and your teachers. Faith that the Bears will win, that the family car will start, that doing the right thing is the way to live.

This is all great stuff. It makes you a great kid whom everybody likes. Someone people can count on. It makes life fun.

But nothing is as important in your life as what you believe about Jesus. To have faith in Jesus is to believe that he is the Son of God. It is to believe in his words of hope and salvation that are written in the Bible.

True faith in Jesus means more than just believing. You live for Jesus. Every day of your life, you do everything for Jesus.

Come up with three things you can do that will show others your faith in Jesus.

TOP SECRET

Read Romans 2:1-4, 16.

One day, God will appoint Jesus to judge everyone's secret thoughts.

Baylor's quarterback was smiling because he had a secret. Even if it were one that nobody would believe.

The Baylor-Texas game of 1974 is part of Baylor lore as the "Miracle on the Brazos." The 12th-ranked Longhorns were favored, and sure enough, they led 24-7 at halftime.

So why was quarterback Neal Jeffrey smiling in the Baylor dressing room at halftime? Head coach Grant Teaff sure didn't like it. "What do you see funny about being down 24-7?" he shouted. That's when Jeffrey let the world in on his secret.

"Coach," he said, still smiling. "We got 'em right where we want 'em." What? How could that be? "They're thinking, 'Same old Baylor,'"

Jeffrey said. "But we're not."

Soon everyone at the game knew Jeffrey's secret. The Bears blocked a punt and scored, and Jeffrey hit wide receiver Ricky Thompson with a 54-yard touchdown bomb. The "Miracle on the Brazos" had begun. Baylor outscored Texas 27-0 in the last half for a 34-24 win.

You probably have some secrets you keep from certain people. Do you tell your sisters and brothers everything? How about your mom and dad? Maybe there's a girl or a boy at school or at church that you really like but you haven't told anyone.

You can keep some secrets from the world. You must never think, though, that you can keep a secret from God. God knows everything. He knows all your mistakes, all your sins, all the bad things you say or think.

But here's something that's not a secret: No matter what God knows about you, he still loves you. Enough to die for you on a cross.

Does it make you feel good or bad that God knows your secrets? Why?

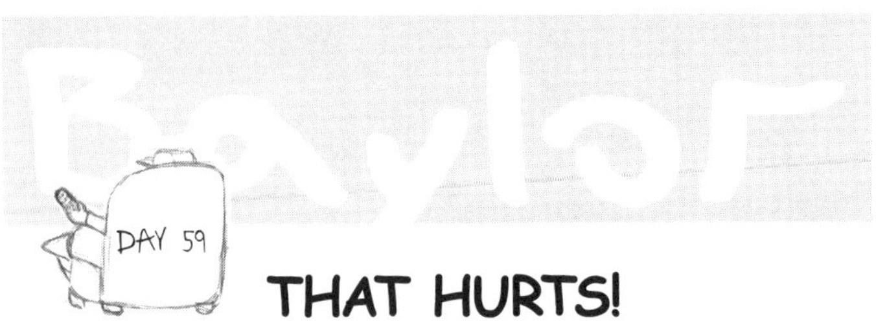

THAT HURTS!

Read 2 Corinthians 1:3-7.

God is the father of all comfort in our pain and our suffering.

He was in such pain he could only hobble onto the field. Still, he pulled off the play that gave Baylor a miracle.

Injuries kept Jack Wilson from being remembered as one of Baylor's greatest athletes ever. He was a star on the track team, a starting guard on the basketball team, and the starting tailback and kicker for the football team.

But injuries dogged him the whole time at Baylor. In 1941, for instance, he missed half of the football season with a kidney injury. When he recovered from that, he sprained an ankle.

Without their star, the team fell to 3-3 by the Texas game. The Horns were ranked No. 1. One writer said they'd beat Baylor so bad that women and children shouldn't watch it.

But Baylor played tough. With 18 seconds to play, Kit Kittrell completed a 19-yard scoring pass to Bill Coleman to make it a 7-6 game. Barely able to walk, Jack Wilson limped out to finish the miracle. His PAT kick was true.

In 1956, that 7-7 tie was voted the greatest upset in the first forty years of the Southwest Conference.

Does a day go by when you don't feel pain? A scrape from a fall on the playground. A blister from your shoes. A bump on the head.

Some pain isn't just physical. Bruises and bumps don't hurt nearly as bad as it does when someone is mean to you.

Jesus knows all about pain. After all, they drove nails into his hands and feet, hung him on two pieces of wood, and stuck a spear in his side. It was an awful, painful way to die.

So when you hurt, you can find comfort in Jesus. He's been there before. He knows all about tears and pain.

Look over your body for bumps, bruises, scratches, and scrapes. Tell how you got each one and how bad it hurt.

UNBELIEVABLE!

Read Hebrews 3:12-14.

Do not have an unbelieving heart that turns you away from God.

The comeback the Bears pulled off against Kansas was just downright unbelievable.

On Nov. 12, 2011, Baylor flat rolled over and died for three quarters against the Jayhawks. Kansas led 24-3 heading into the last period.

Robert Griffin III broke loose for a 49-yard touchdown run, but Baylor was still 14 points down. It looked bad when a Kansas punt left the Bears sitting at their own 2-yard line.

Unbelievably, they drove 98 yards to score with 7:58 left to play. They trailed only 24-17.

A punt set Baylor back to its 20. Then RGIII tossed what he called "the best worst pass I ever threw in my life." It was "a wounded duck that seemed to flutter in the wind forever." But Tevin Reese hauled in that wounded duck and took it 67 yards to tie the game at 24.

It was on to overtime. Both teams scored but Kansas went for two and the win. Joe Williams batted a pass away. 'It was the biggest comeback I've ever been a part of," Griffin said of the unbelievable 31-30 Baylor win.

You know, it doesn't really matter much if you don't believe in some things. Like magic. Or dragons. Or that a four-leaf clover can bring you good luck.

But it matters a whole lot that you believe in Jesus as the Son of God. Some people say that Jesus was a good man and a good teacher and that's all.

They are wrong, and their unbelief is bad for them. God doesn't fool around with people who don't believe in Jesus as their Savior. He locks them out of Heaven forever.

If you believe, you'll go to Heaven one day and be happy with God and Jesus.

Talk to your parents about some things you don't believe in and some things you do believe in and why.

TAKE A CHANCE

Read Matthew 4:18-22.

"Come. Follow me," Jesus said. They left their nets and followed him.

Don Trull took a chance on a school he'd never heard of. It worked out right well.

College recruiters weren't lining up to have Trull play quarterback for them in 1959. But Baylor head coach John Bridgers liked what he saw. He invited the youngster to come to Waco. Trull took a chance and went, though he had never even heard of Baylor. He liked the campus and Coach Bridgers and took another chance. He committed to Baylor.

For a while, it looked as though he had made a mistake. He was fourth or fifth string on the freshman team. "I had been on the bottom of the barrel before," he said, "but not four bottoms down." He wanted to leave, but his parents told him to take a chance and stay.

It was a good thing. His last two seasons in Waco, Trull rewrote the Baylor record books. He was All-America in 1963 and went on to a pro career. He was inducted into the College Football Hall of Fame in 2013.

Have you ever thought that like Don Trull you take chances every day? You risk getting hurt every time you play at PE, go swimming, or play paint ball. You risk getting a bad grade with every test you take. You still take chances, though, figuring whatever you get is worth it.

Simon Peter, Andrew, James, and John took a chance. A big one! They fished to make a living, and they gave that up to follow this wandering preacher they didn't even know.

Jesus wants you to take that same chance with your life by giving it to him. What have you got to lose? Nothing really. What have you got to gain? Everlasting life with God.

That's something worth taking a chance on.

Write a short story about Jesus coming by your house and calling you as he did the four fishermen.

PLEASE!

Read Matthew 7:7-8.

Ask and it will be given to you.
Search, and you will find.

Kim Mulkey wanted to stay home so badly that she got down on her knees and begged. Then she went to Waco.

Mulkey today is "the undisputed queen of women's basketball in Texas." Since she took over the Baylor program in 2000, the Lady Bears have never won fewer than 21 games. They have also won two national titles.

In 2000, she didn't want to leave La. Tech even when Baylor offered her the head coaching job. She had been at the school for 19 years. Ruston, La., was her home.

The school offered her the head coaching job, but she wanted a five-year contract to give her enough time. They said four years.

In the president's office, she begged him for

five years with tears running down her face. She suddenly realized she had sunk as low as she could go. She wiped her face, stood up, and went to a phone. She called Baylor and took the job. "Sometimes you thank God for unanswered prayers," she later said.

You've probably seen scruffy looking people with handmade signs at interstate exits begging for money. In a city, a beggar might run up, spray your car's windshield, and expect your parents to give him money.

As it was with Kim Mulkey, begging is an act of last resort. You beg when it's all you've got. You are powerless, at the complete mercy of the one you're begging from.

Do you know that's the way it is with you and God? He has all the power; you have none. He can do with you whatever he wants to.

But he doesn't require you to beg him for something. You pray; you just ask — because he loves you.

Make a sign like a beggar does and beg your parents for money. Then ask God to forgive your sins. Which is harder?

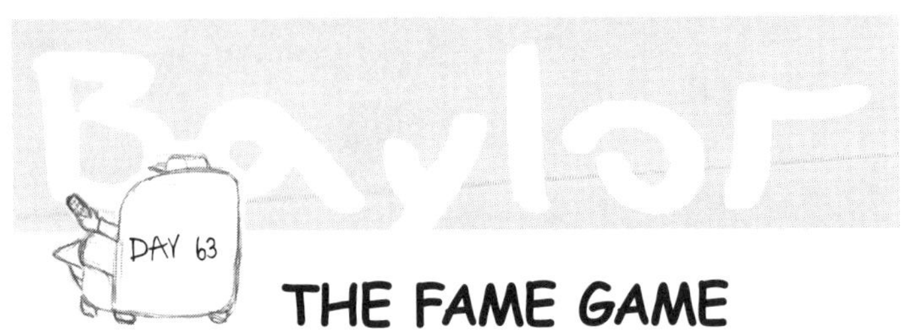

THE FAME GAME

Read 1 Kings 10:23-25.

Solomon was so famous people all over the world wanted to meet him.

Already famous at Baylor, Darryl Middleton dreamed of being famous playing pro basketball. He didn't know he'd have to travel halfway around the world to do it.

Middleton was a star at Baylor from 1985-88. He was inducted into the Baylor Athletic Hall of Fame in 2010.

He was drafted by the Atlanta Hawks in 1988 but couldn't crack the roster. A coach asked him if he was interested in playing ball in Turkey. Middleton didn't even know they played basketball there, but his wife and he headed overseas. He was the league MVP.

Middleton returned to the states, but again he couldn't catch on with an NBA team. So he went to Italy and played ball.

Middleton never really came home again. Over the next 25 years, he played for a lot of European teams. He changed clubs 15 times in five countries. Three times he was the MVP of the Spanish league. From Spain to Russia, he played for ten championship teams.

Playing until he was 47, he was one of the most famous of Europe's American players

A lot of grown-ups want to be famous like the people on TV or in the movies. Fame just means that complete strangers know your name and face. Baylor's football players are like that. A lot of people whom they've never met know their names and what they look like.

Are you famous? The answer may surprise you. The truth is that you are famous where it really counts. Baylor's football players may not know you, but God does. God knows your name, what you look like, and even what size shoe you wear. You are famous in Heaven where God and the angels live.

Name some people you think are famous. Was Jesus on the list?

FOR THE FUN OF IT

Read Nehemiah 8:1-3, 9-12.

The people ate and drank and celebrated with great joy.

A lot of folks didn't like the way John Bridgers coached football because he made it fun.

Bridgers was the head Bear from 1959-68. Three of his teams went to bowl games.

In 1962, the alumni wanted him fired. They said he was too soft on his players and kept players who weren't good enough. Surprisingly, Bridgers said they were right.

He never cut a player from the team just because he wasn't good enough. He never shouted at his players or criticized them in front of other players at practice. He believed the players should laugh and have fun even while they were practicing.

Bridgers refused to bench his players when they made mistakes in games. "They're college

Bears

boys," he said, "not paid professionals."

His players loved him, of course, and played hard for him. Even the teachers at Baylor liked him, which was unusual for a football coach.

He kept his job even though — unlike most coaches — he believed football should be fun.

A lot of people think that Christians should always be out trying to keep folks from having fun. But that is so, so wrong.

The Israelites cried when Ezra read them God's law because they had failed God. But Nehemiah told them not to cry, to go throw a party instead! Go eat and drink with your buddies, he said. That shows you right there how God feels about having fun. He's for it.

It should be that way for you. Having fun is a form of celebrating all that God has given you, which is everything you have. Especially your salvation in Jesus.

To live for Jesus is to know the fun in living.

Do something that is so much fun it makes you laugh. Remember that's how God wants you to live.

DEAD WRONG

Read Matthew 26:14-16; 27:1-5.

Judas was ashamed and sad because he had betrayed Jesus.

The rings the Baylor players got for winning the 2012 Holiday Bowl have the wrong score on them. Or do they?

In the bowl game, the 7-5 Bears took on 17th-ranked UCLA, which was favored. That was wrong. By halftime, Baylor led 35-10. During the game, Nick Florence broke Robert Griffin III's school single-season passing record.

The Bears' domination led to a final score of . . . Well, that's a problem. Baylor led 49-19 and UCLA scored as time ran out. Replays showed, however, that the UCLA runner never crossed the goal line.

Head coach Art Briles wanted to challenge the touchdown. He found out, though, that the replay officials had already packed their gear and left. So UCLA kept the touchdown and the PAT to make the final score 49-26.

Briles thought that was the wrong score. So when he ordered rings for everybody to celebrate the win, he put a 49-19 score on them.

Everybody's wrong at some time or other. Maybe you walked into the wrong classroom at school. How many times have you come up with the wrong answer on a test?

Here's a secret: Even grown-ups are wrong. All the adults from either Baylor or UCLA were wrong about the final score of that bowl game.

Think about Judas. He turned Jesus over to folks who wanted to kill him. Can anything be more wrong than that?

Judas felt sorry about what he did to Jesus, but it didn't help. That's because he tried to make it all right himself instead of asking God to forgive him. He was dead wrong this time.

When you do something wrong, you make it worse if you don't pray to God for forgiveness.

Think of something you did wrong today. Ask God to forgive you. How do you feel?

NO GUARANTEES

Read James 4:13-15.

You don't even know what will happen tomorrow.

Steffanie Blackmon thought she was light-headed because she hadn't eaten very much that day. That was right before she collapsed, her heart stopped, and the doctors said she wouldn't live.

In 2004, Steffanie was a junior All-American center for the Baylor women's basketball team. She was riding with her twin sister in the car when she suddenly had a seizure.

At a hospital, her heart stopped more than once. Doctors told the family they probably should call in their pastor.

But Steffanie lived. Three days later, she was released from the hospital. After that one incident, she picked right up with her life. She was a key part of the 2005 national champs.

Bears

She never received any special attention from the trainers. They just made sure she had plenty of food and water.

Her brush with death drew the family closer together. "When Steffanie got sick, the love we had for one another showed," said her twin sister. "I didn't want to lose her."

A guarantee is a promise that something will happen or someone will do something. As Steffanie Blackmon's brush with death shows, life has no guarantees. That means life doesn't promise you anything — including tomorrow.

You don't know what's going to happen two hours from now. Or if there will be a tomorrow. That's because your life is in God's hands, not yours, which is a good place for it to be. God is in control of your life; you're not.

So you live today for God and take care of tomorrow by giving your life to Jesus. When you do, forever with God is guaranteed.

Find a newspaper ad with a guarantee. Does it sound good? As good as God's guarantee of eternal life in Heaven?

KEEP IT SIMPLE

Read 1 John 1:5-10.

If we admit to God that we have sinned, he will forgive us.

The record shows that Baylor boss Art Briles can coach a quarterback. He has a formula for success: Keep it simple.

One *ESPN* writer said, "The Bears have been able to plug in one quarterback after another" without missing a beat. It's true.

The beat started with Robert Griffin III, who set a school record for yards passing. Then senior Nick Florence stepped up and broke Griffin's record in 2012 with 4,309 yards passing. He left and along came junior Bryce Petty. He accounted for 46 touchdowns in 2013 and 35 in 2014 and led the Bears to two straight conference titles. Both years Baylor led the country in points per game.

Briles keeps the offense rolling by keeping it

Bears

simple for his quarterbacks. They don't even have a playbook to learn! They watch videos and practice a lot. It's that simple.

Even in the games, it's simple. The QB's rarely read the defenses and change the plays. A running back or tight end does it.

Why so simple? "We try to ease the load on the quarterbacks," Briles said. And it works.

Being a kid isn't simple. You have to juggle school and homework, baseball or basketball, church and Sunday school, dancing class, 4-H, and anything else that comes along. You have to do your chores at the house like making up your bed and taking out the garbage.

But, you know, life is really pretty simple. Just like Coach Briles shows with his quarterbacks. You keep it simple by putting the basic stuff first. You worship God, love your family, honor your teachers, and always do your best.

That's means you're obeying God in the way you live. It's simple — and it's the best.

It's simple: Ask God for forgiveness of our sins and we get it. Why do you think God made it so easy?

SIZE MATTERS

Read Luke 19:1-10.

Zacchaeus wanted to see Jesus, but he was so short, he had to climb a tree.

Size doesn't always matter in sports. So said Lady Bears head basketball coach Kim Mulkey. Nina Davis proves her point.

Davis was a high school All-America, but most college coaches still didn't think much of her. They didn't like her size or her shot.

Her size? She is 5'11. Her shot? A strange one "that comes almost directly from the top of her head." Coaches saw a player too small to play forward with a shot that wouldn't let her play guard.

Not Mulkey. "If you can play, you can play," she said about Davis. She put Davis at forward, meaning she played against taller players. It didn't matter. She played "with the soul of

Bears

someone 6-4" and scored 28 points in her second college game.

This player who was the wrong size was the Big 12 Freshman of the Year in 2014. In 2015, she was the league's Player of the Year.

Everybody seems to think bigger is better. Bigger houses, bigger burgers. You even super-size your fries. You just can't wait to grow up some so you can be taller and bigger, can you?

But, you know, size didn't matter to Jesus. Salvation came to the house of a bad man who was so short he had to climb a tree to even see Jesus. Zacchaeus was a big shot because he was rich, but that didn't matter to Jesus either. Zacchaeus was saved because he was sorry for all the wrong things he had done. He changed his life as a result.

The same is true for you. What matters to Jesus is the size of your heart, the one you give to him.

Look at some of your old pictures.
Have you grown much?
Have you grown in your love for Jesus?

ON CALL

Read 1 Samuel 3:1-10.

Samuel said, "Speak, Lord. I'm listening."

Nick Florence was called on to make a sacrifice for his team few athletes are ever asked to do.

When the Bears played Texas Tech in 2011, they led 31-28 at halftime. But Baylor was in real trouble. Shortly before the break, Robert Griffin III suffered a concussion.

Backup Bryce Petty was the obvious choice to replace him. But then head coach Art Briles made a really radical decision. He turned to Florence. What was the problem? He was being redshirted. (A college player may play only four seasons. If he is redshirted, he does not play at all, and it doesn't count as one of his years.) Playing the last half meant Florence would lose the whole season.

What did he tell Briles? "Whatever I can do to help the team, I'll do it," he said. "We need you, Nick," his coach said.

Florence answered the call. He played the last half and led the Bears to a 66-42 win. He didn't play another snap that season. His entire junior season consisted of two quarters.

You may have answered the call that time a coach needed you to play a new position in a game. Or when your teacher calls on you.

Did you know God, too, is calling you? God wants you to do something for him with your life. That sounds scary, doesn't it?

But answering God's call doesn't mean you have to be a preacher. Or be a missionary in some way-off place where they never heard of macaroni and cheese, video games, or Baylor.

God calls you to serve him right where you are. At school. At home. On the playground. You answer God's call when you do everything for his glory and not your own.

Talk and pray with your parents about what God may be calling you to do and how you can answer that call.

NO EXCUSES!

Read Luke 9:59-62.

If you start to follow Jesus and then make excuses not to serve him, you are not fit for Heaven.

Isaiah Austin wouldn't make any excuse that would keep him from playing basketball. Not even being blind in one eye.

When he was 12, Austin was struck in the right eye by a thrown baseball. Doctors said that he could go blind in the eye at any time.

They were right. In the eighth grade, Austin pulled off a routine dunk. (He was already 6-7 in the eighth grade!) He suddenly realized he could see only red out of his right eye.

Surgeries followed, but he wound up totally blind in the eye. He mother told him, "You can touch lives or you can be a quitter." Austin chose not to quit.

He changed the way he played, moving his

head all the time so he could see more of the court. He received a scholarship to Baylor in 2012. He didn't tell the Bear head coach or his teammates about his eye until after he had arrived. He became a star.

"You can make it your excuse, or you can make it your story," Austin said.

You've made some excuses before, haven't you? What excuse did you use when you didn't do your homework? Have you ever said you felt bad so you didn't have to do something?

Lots of folks make excuses when we don't like the way things are going. Or when stuff gets too hard. Or we fail at something.

We do it with our faith life, too. We say the Bible's too hard to read. The weather's too pretty to be shut up in church. Or praying in public is downright embarrassing.

But, you know, Jesus died for you without making any excuses. The least you can do is live for him with no excuses.

What excuse did you use the last time you missed church? Do you think God thought it was a good one?

Baylor

NOTES

(by devotion number)

1 On Thanksgiving Day, 1895, . . . so they did.: Alan J. Lefever, *The History of Baylor Sports* (Waco: Baylor University Press, 2013), p. 27.
1 Those games among the . . . but was soon dropped.: Lefever, p. 29.
2 against Oklahoma, she dived . . . letting her play on.: David Pond, "Seeing the Light," *Sharing the Victory Magazine*, March/April 2012, http://archives.fca.org/vsItemDisplay.
2 "It's part of my . . . have to adapt to it.": Irv Moss, "Colorado Classics," *The Denver Post*, Dec. 26, 2012, http://www.denverpost.com/ci_22259767/legacy-high-alum-melissa-jones-was-an-inspirational-athlete-at-baylor/article.
3 At the last minute, . . . a shoeshine kit.: "Program History," *2013 Baylor Football Media Almanac*, p. 89, http://www.baylorbears.com/sports/m-footbl/13-media-almanac.html.
4 He was Canadian and . . . they keep talking about?": Nick Eatman, *Art Briles Looking Up: My Journey from Tragedy to Triumph* (Chicago: Triumph Books, 2013), pp. 239-240.
5 a "once-in-a-generation" of the Baylor football program.: "Robert Griffin III," *baylorbears.com*, http;//www.baylorbears.com/sports-m-footbl/mtt/griffiniii_robert00.html.
5 When Baylor recruited him, . . . Griffin said forget it.: Pablo S. Torre, "Back of All Trades," *Sports Illustrated*, Sept. 26, 2011, http://www.sportsillustrated.cnn.com/vault/article/magazine/MAG1190636/index.htm.
6 Ganaway wasn't sure he . . . hard and get ready. Eatman, p. 257.
6 Each day of the week . . . Do you feel it? You should.": Eatman, p. 258.
7 "It was amazing, considering he only took three jumps,": "Obi Leaps for Bears," *Waco Tribune-Herald*, March 16, 2014, http://www.wacotrib.com/sports/baylor/baylor_track_and_field/obi-leaps-for-bears-st-national-title-since/article.
7 "I almost wanted to . . . last jump was done.": "Obi Wins NCAA Indoor Triple Jump Crown," *baylorbears.com*, March 15, 2014, http://www.baylorbears.com/sports/c-track/recaps/031514aab.html.
8 "This was the year the unbelievable became believable at Baylor.": John Werner, "Afterword," *Year of the Bear* (Waco: Pediment Publishing, 2012), p. 139.
9 Four minutes into the . . . had beaten Oklahoma State.: John Werner, "Trophy Case," *Waco Tribune-Herald*, Dec. 8, 2013, http://www.wacotrib.com/sports/baylor/football/trophy-case-bears-brave-bitter-cold-for-big-title-bcs/article.
9 Before the game ended . . . presented the championship trophy.: Werner, "Trophy Case."
10 "You're dadgum right we . . . no track around it.": John Werner, 'Floyd Casey's 1st Tenants Share Tales of 1950 Triumphs," *Waco Tribune-Herald*, Aug. 31, 2013, www.wacotrib.com/sports/baylor/football/floyd-casey-s-st-tenants-share-tales-of-triumphs/article.
10 "the Baylor players had . . . could hardly believe it,": Werner, "Floyd Casey's 1st Tenants."
11 In 2007, the head Bear . . . horse ranch for himself.: Eatman, pp. 225-26.
12 Right before Christmas in . . . the good of the team.: John Werner, "DE McAllister Showing Doubters Wrong at Baylor," *Waco Tribune-Herald*, Oct. 5, 2013, http://www.waco trib.com/sports/football/de-mcallister-showing-doubters-wrong-at-baylor/article.
13 Early on, Jones saw . . . "The Smiling Assassin.": Janet Goreham, "Keeping Up with the Jones," *Sharing the Victory Magazine*, May 8, 2009, http://www.sharingthevictory.com/vsItemDisplay.1sp&objectID=AC8A85E2-99A5-4CD7.
14 "the biggest win for . . . bowl eligible at Baylor,": Eatman, p. 249.
15 The way she looked . . . no way to explain it.: Brice Cherry, "Lady Bears' 'Miracle' Mariah," *Waco Tribune-Herald*, Nov. 21, 2012, http://www.wacotrib.com/sports/baylor/brice-cherry-lady-bears-miracle-mariah-chandler-ever-grateful-for/article.
16 He called him to the . . . clippers for several months.: Eatman, pp. 273-74.
17 The TCU record book . . . about the final score.": "Program History," *2013 Baylor Football Media Almanac*, , p. 86, http://www.baylorbears.com/sports/m-footbl/13-media-almanac.html.
18 "All week we believed . . . surprised when it happened.": Will Parchman, "K-State's Heisman, BCS Title Hopes Cast Aside," *Waco Tribune-Herald*, Nov. 18, 2012, http://www.wacotrib.com/sports/byalor/will-parchman-k-state-s-heisman-bcs-title-hopes-cast/

article.
19 He told his players . . . and 248 Baylor fans.: Grant Teaff, "High Stakes Yield Cheers at 'Big House,'" *Waco Tribune-Herald*, Oct. 5, 2013, http://www.wacotrib.com/sports/baylor/football/grant-teaff-remembers-higher-stakes-yield-cheers-at-big-house/article.
20 he had barely taken any snaps at practice.: Eatman, p. 241.
20 the head coach wanted . . . that was Florence's number, too.: Eatman, p. 243.
21 "It was probably one of . . . in the fourth quarter.: John Werner, "Bears Anxious to Disprove Road Woes," *Waco Tribune-Herald*, Oct. 12, 2013, http://www.wacotrib.com/sports/byalor/football/bears-anxious-to-disprove-road-woes/article.
21 "We want to prove to people we can win on the road,": Werner, "Bears Anxious."
22 missed it by one spot. . . . not have ever played football.": Eatman, pp. 232-33.
23 Broyles was in the . . . but which ones?": "Program History," p. 88.
24 Head coach Grant Teaff knew . . . never stand again.: Grant Teaff, "1980 Team Turned Setback into a Comeback," *Waco Tribune-Herald*, Oct. 28, 2013, http://www.wacotrib.com/sports/baylor/football/grant-teaff-remembers-team-turned-setback-into-a-comeback/article.
25 With two outs in the . . . that 1998 team at the game,: Laura A Cadena, "Longest Softball Game to End," *The Lariat, Sept.* 14, 1995, http://www.baylor.edu/lariatarchives/news.php?action+stoty&story=8736.
26 Levi wasn't too happy . . . in Jesus was Baylor.: Max Olson "Baylor Finds Breakout Weapon in Norwood," *ESPN.com*, Nov. 19, 2013, http://www.espn.go.com/blog/ncfnation/post/_/id/88654/baylor-finds-breakout-weapon-in-norwood.
27 Baylor's star left end . . . "Mr Fouts' strip act.": "Program History," p. 86.
28 "a big, big, game for us.": John Werner, "Bears Rein in Mustangs with Solid Defensive Effort," *Waco Tribune-Herald*, Sept. 3, 2012, http://www.wacotrib.com/sports/football/baylor/bear-rein-in-mustangs-with solid-defensive effort/article.
28 "We did that.": Werner, "Bears Rein in Mustangs with Solid Defensive Effort."
29 The Gators started talking . . . start talking about Florida.": Brice Cherry, "Baylor Lady Bears Are Swatting Everyone's Best Shot," *Waco Tribune-Herald*, March 20, 2012, http://www.wacotrib.com/sports/baylor/baylor-lady-bears-are-swatting-everyone-s-best-shot/article.
29 During the on-court . . . "go win it all.": Cherry, "Baylor Lady Bears Are Swatting.'
30 In August 1985, a heat . . . but not that hot,": Grant Teaff, "Memories Extend Beyond Field of Play," *Waco Tribune-Herald*, Nov. 7, 2013, http://www.wacotrib.com/sports/baylor/football/grant-teaff/memories-extend-beyond-field-of-play/article.
31 the Baylor fans and players . . . Baylor's two bear cub mascots.: Dave Campbell, "The Legendary Texas Sportswriter Recalls Some of Baylor's Best Games of the 1950s," *baylorbears.com*, Dec. 9, 2013, http://www.baylorbears.com/sports/m-footbl/spec-rel/120913aab.html.
31 By then, the stolen . . . back seat to shreds.: Campbell, "The Legendary Texas Sports writer."
32 Buildings hit a speeding . . . struck the rear of the bus.: Lefever, p. 93.
32 Ten of the twenty-one . . . the ten who died.: "The Immortal Ten," *baylorbears.com: Traditions*, baylorbears.com/trads/bay-immortal-10.html.
33 Robinson represented the team . . . from Texas, not California.: John Henry, "Jack Robinson Returns to London," *Star-Telegram*, July 25, 2012, http://www.star-telegram.com/2012/07/25/4126689/jack-robinson-returns-to-london.html.
34 Baylor head coach Art Briles . . . a pair of Superman socks.: John Werner, "Robert Griffin III Wins Baylor's First Heisman Trophy," *Year of the Bear*, p. 25.
34 During an interview with . . . a pair of Elmo socks.: Regina Dennis, "Heisman Winner's Superman Socks Soar in Popularity," *Year of the Bear*, p. 28.
34 At various times, he . . . SpongeBob SquarePants.: Lance Madden, "Robert Griffin III, Adidas Have a Lot of Sock Swag," *Forbes*, Sept. 21, 2012, http://www.forbes.com/sites/lancemadden/2012/09/21/robert-griffin-iii-adidas-have-a-lot-of-sock-swag/.
36 Some local folks wanted . . . Texas coach never came.: "Program History," p. 87.
36 A whole bunch of . . . he stood up in Hillsboro.: "Program History," p. 87.
37 Robertson didn't even think . . . until her senior year." Graham Hays, "Makenzie, Kim Make Perfect Team," *ESPN*, Feb. 13, 2014, http://www.espn.go.com/womens-college-basketball/story/_/id10437949.

38 "I want to play . . . short of the first down.: Grant Teaff, "Final Games End, But Memories Last," *Waco Tribune-Herald*, Dec. 7, 2013, http://www.wacotrib.com/sports/baylor/football/grant-teaff-remembes-final-games-end-but-memories-last.

39 "We were a bit looser," . . . The dugout went nuts.: Kevin Sherrington, "Late Mickey Sullivan Kept Baylor Baseball on Top," *Dallas Morning News*, March 21, 2012, http://www.dallasnews.com/sports/columnists/kevin-sherrington/20120331-sherrington-late-mickey-sullivan-kept-baylor-on-top-with-casual-style.ece.

40 Before the 1978 game, the . . . didn't call for volunteers.": Grant Teaff, "Wriggly Stunt Helps 1978 Baylor Team Turn Corner," *Waco Tribune-Herald*, Oct. 12, 2013, http://www.wacotrib.com/sports/baylor/football/grant-teaff-wriggly-stunt-helps-baylor-team-turn-corner/article.

41 Head coach Art Briles stamped . . . "StorkThe Dork.": David Ubben, "Baylor Continuing to 'Shock' the World," *FoxSports.com*, Nov. 12, 2013, http://www/msn.foxsports.com/southwest/story/baylor-continuing-to-shock-the-world-111213.

41 He was born when . . . shortened to just "Shock.": Ubben, "Baylor Continuing to 'Shock.'"

42 everybody asked the question . . . team Baylor had become?: John Werner, "Baylor Men Knock Off No. 3," *Waco Tribune-Herald*, March 24, 2014, http://www.wacrotrib.com/sports/baylor/mens-basketball/baylor-men-knock-off-no-creighton-to-advance/article.

43 Lackey could find any . . . before he left campus.: John Werner, "New Baylor Linebacker," *Waco Tribune-Herald*, Sept. 14, 2012, http://www.wacotrib.com/sports/baylor/new-baylor-linebacker-showing-he-only-needed-chance/article.

44 At halftime, some Baylor . . . snapped to attention.: Lefever, p. 33.

44 One Aggie, though, was . . . before it all got worse.: Lefever, p. 36.

45 "We're getting embarrassed on national television,": Grant Wahl, "Choice Words," *Sports Illustrated*, Dec. 12, 2005, http://www/sportsillustrated.cnn.com/vault/article/magazine/MAG1114641/index.htm.

45 Mulkey first said nothing. . . . found their groove again.: Wahl, "Choice Words."

46 When the job came open, . . . on Baylor or his quarterback,: Eatman, p. 245.

47 When reporters first tried . . . even took a class.: John Werner, ""Baylor Receiver Lets Game Do His Talking," *Waco Tribune-Herald*, Oct. 15, 2010, http://www.wacotrib.com/sports/baylor/baylor-receiver-lets-game-do-his-talking/article.

48 "That's the most tired I've ever been,": Stephen Baylor, "Baylor K Aaron Jones Kicking Up NCAA Record," *AP College Football*, Nov. 19, 2013, collegefootball.ap.org/article/baylor-k-aaron-jones-kicking-ncaa-record.

50 He needed to change the . . . "We'll win,": Grant Teaff, "Confident Bears Showed the Difference in '72," *Waco Tribune-Herald*, Sept. 7, 2013, http://www.wacotrib.com/sports/baylor/football/grant-teaff-confident-bears-showed-the-difference-in/article.

51 Before the 1910 game, . . . Texas declined the offer: "Program History, p. 86.

52 He was a freshman . . . got a scholarship.: Jeff Brown, "Spotlight: Cyril Richardson," *baylorbears.com*, Oct. 5, 2013, http://www.baylorbears.com/sports/m-footbl/mtt/richardson_cyril100.html.

53 Campbell began playing baseball . . . with its Christian environment.: Brice Cherry, "Baylor Infielder Shrugs Off Junior Slump," *Waco Tribune-Herald*, May 21, 2010, http://www.wacotrib.com/sports/baylor/baylor-infielder-shrugs-off-junior-slump/article.

53 "It was very frustrating," . . . a better ballplayer.": Cherry, "Baylor Infielder Shrugs."

54 His father was gassed . . . until I was 16,": John Werner, "Baylor Legend Elkins Helped Shape Future," *Waco Tribune-Herald*, Nov. 14, 2009, http://www.wacotrib.com/sports/baylor/football/baylor-legend-elkins-helped-shape-future-of-college-football/article.

55 Sue Turner called the . . . they played for Baylor.: Summer Morgan, "A Baylor Bearette," MYPlainview.com, April 7, 2012, http;//www.myplainview.com/sports/article.

55 As late as 1979, . . . to support the team.: Helen Cho, "The Baylor University Women's Basketball Team," *Texas Monthly,* June 2005, http://www.texasmonthly.com/content/texas-history-101-51.

56 Fans "stampeded out of the . . . headline "Bowl Bound.": John Werner, "Bowl Eligibility Only Footnote," *Waco Tribune-Herald*, Oct. 20, 2013, http://www.wacotrib.com/sports/baylor/football/bowl-eligibility-only-footnote-as-bears-dismantle-cyclones/article.

57 Rumor said more than . . . and [took] the job,": Grant Teaff, "Step of Faith Led to Most Unexpected Landing Spot," *Waco Tribune-Herald*, Aug. 31, 2013, http://www.wacotrib.com/sports/baylor/football/grant-teaff-step-of-faith-led-to-most-unexpected-landing/article.

58 "What do you see funny . . . "But we're not.": Grant Teaff, "2 Seasons That Changed Baylor Football Forever," *Waco Tribune-Herald*, Sept. 22, 2013, http://www.wacotrib.com/sports/baylor/football/grant-teaff-seasons-that-changed-baylor-football-forever/article.

59 One writer said they'd . . . shouldn't watch it.: Dave Campbell, "Veteran Writer Remembers Baylor Great Jack Wilson," *baylorbears.com*, April 25, 2001, http://www.baylorbears.com/sports/m-footbl/spec-rel/042501aaa.html.

59 In 1956, that tie . . . the Southwest Conference.": Campbell, "Veteran Writer Remembers."

60 "the best worst pass . . . in the wind forever.": John Werner, "Last Year's Baylor Comeback," *Waco Tribune-Herald*, Nov. 2, 2012, http://www.wacotrib.com/sports/baylor/john-werner-last-year-s-baylor-comeback/article.

61 College recruiters weren't lining . . . take a chance and stay.: John Werner, "Hall of Fame Profile," *Waco Tribune-Herald*, Jan. 24, 2014, http://www.wacotrib.com/sports/baylor/football/hall-of-fame-profile-all-american-qb-don-trull/article.

62 "the undisputed queen of women's basketball in Texas.": Barry Horn, "Baylor's Kim Mulkey Is Fierce," *Dallas Morning News*, March 9, 2012, http://www.dallasnews.com/sports/college-sports/baylor-bears/20120309-baylor-s-kim-mulkey-is-fierce-loving-and-loyal-but-dont-get-on-her-bad-side.ece.

62 The school offered her the . . . for unanswered prayers,": Horn, "Baylor's Kim Mulkey."

63 A coach asked him . . . ten championship teams.: Sam Borden, "The Basketball Player's Guide to the (European) Galaxy," *New York Times*, Jan. 12, 2014, http://www.nytimes.com/2014/01/13/sports/basketball/teh-basketball-players-guide-to-the-european-galaxy.html.

64 In 1962, the alumni . . . at Baylor liked him,: Morton Shamik, "A Coach Even the Faculty Likes," *Sports Illustrated*, Nov. 18, 1963, http://www.sportsillustrated.cnn.com/vault/article/magazine/MAG1075384/index.htm.

65 Replays, showed, however, . . . a 49-19 score on them.: Eatman, pp. 280-81.

66 Steffanie Blackmon thought she . . . want to lose her.": Calvin Watkins, "Ordeal Brings Blackmon Sisters Closer," *The Dallas Morning News*, April 3, 2005.

67 "The Bears have been . . . without missing a beat.: Mark Schlabach, "Briles' Offense Built Around Each QB," ESPN, Oct 16, 2013, http://www.espn.go.com/college-football/story/_/id/9833069/baylor-coach-art-briles-builds-offense-quarterback.

67 They don't even have a . . . load on the quarterbacks,": Schlabach, "Briles' Offense."

68 Size doesn't always matter in sports.: Jason Orts, "Lady Bears Freshman Nina Davis Overlooked No More," *Waco Tribune-Herald*, Feb. 9, 2014, http://www.wacotribu.com/sports/baylor/lady_bears_basketball/lady-bears-freshman-nina-davis-overlooked-no-more/article.

68 most college coaches didn't . . . soul of someone 6'4": Orts, "Lady Bears Freshman Nina Davis Overlooked No More."

69 "Whatever I can do . . . "We need you, Nick,": Eatman, p. 261.

70 When he was 12, . . . make it your story,": Stephen Hawkins, "Blind Eye No Excuse for Baylor's Isaiah Austin," *boston.com*, Feb. 13, 2014, http://www.boston.com/sports/colleges/mens-basketball/2014/02/13-blind-eye-no-excuse-for-baylor-isaiah-austin.

SOURCES

"Baylor Survives Late Blunder." *Dallas Morning News*. 17 Feb. 2014. http://www.dallasnews.com/sports/college-sports/baylor-bears/20140217/baylor-survives-late-blunder.

Borden, Sam. "The Basketball Player's Guide to the (European) Galaxy." *New York Times*. 12 Jan. 2014. http://www.nytimes.com/2014/01/13/sports/basketball/the-basketball-players-guide-to-the-european-galaxy.html.

Brown, Jeff. "Spotlight: Cyril Richardson." *baylorbears.com*. 5 Oct. 2013. http://www.baylorbears.com/sports/m-footbl/mtt/richardson_cyril100.html.

Cadena, Laura A. "Longest Softball Game to End." *The Lariat*. 14 Sept. 1995. http://www.bayloredu./lariatarchives/news.php?action+story&story=8736.

Campbell, Dave. "The Legendary Texas Sportswriter Recalls Some of Baylor's Best Games of the 1950s." *baylorbears.com*. 9 Dec. 2013. http://www.baylorbears.com/sports/m-footbl/spec-rel/120913aab.html.

-----. "Veteran Writer Remembers Baylor Great Jack Wilson." *baylorbears.com*. 25 April 2001. http://www.baylorbears.com/sports/m-footbl/spec-rel/042501aaa.html.

Cherry, Brice. "Baylor Infielder Shrugs Off Junior Slump." *Waco Tribune-Herald*. 21 May 2010. http://www.wacotrib.com/sports/baylor/baylor-infielder-shrugs-off-junior-slump/article.

-----. "Lady Bears Are Swatting Everyone's Best Shot. *Waco Tribune-Herald*. 20 March 2012. http://www/wacotrib.com/sports/baylor/baylor-lady-bears-are-swatting-everyone-s-best-shots/article.

-----. "Lady Bears' 'Miracle' Mariah." *Waco Tribune-Herald*. 21 Nov. 2012. http://www.wacotrib.com/sports/baylor-brice-cherry-lady-bears-miracle-mariah-chandler-ever-grateful-for/article.

Cho, Helen. "The Baylor University Women's Basketball Team Has Come a Long Way." *Texas Monthly*. June 2005. http://www.texasmonthly.com/content/texas-history-101-51.

Dennis, Regina. "Heisman Winner's Superman Socks Soar in Popularity." *Year of the Bear: The Winningest Year in College Sports History*. Waco: Pediment Publishing, 2012. 27-28.

Eatman, Nick. *Art Briles Looking Up: My Journey from Tragedy to Triumph*. Chicago: Triumph Books, 2013.

Goreham, Janet. "Keeping Up with the Jones." *Sharing the Victory Magazine*. 8 May 2009. http://www.sharingthevictory.com/vsItemDisplay.1sp&objectID=AC8A85E2-99A5-4CD7.

Hawkins, Stephen. "Baylor K Aaron Jones Kicking Up NCAA Record." *AP College Football*. 19 Nov. 2013. collegefootball.ap.org/article/baylor-k-aaron-jones-kicking-ncaa-record.

-----. "Blind Eye No Excuse for Baylor's Isaiah Austin." *boston.com*. 13 Feb. 2014. http://www.boston.com/sports/colleges/mens-basketball/2014/02/13-blind-eye-no-excuse-for-baylor-isaiah-austin.

Hays, Gram. "Makenzie, Kim Make Perfect Team." *ESPN*. 13 Feb. 2014. http://www/espn.go.com/womens-college-basketball/story/_/id10437949.

Henry, John. "Jack Robinson Returns to London." *Star-Telegram*. 25 July 2012. http://www.star-telegram.com/2012/07/25/4126689/jack-robinson-returns-to-london.html.

Horn, Barry. "Baylor's Kim Mulkey Is Fierce, Loving and Loyal, But Don't Get on Her Bad Side." *Dallas Morning News*. 9 March 2012. http://www.dallasnews.com/sports/college-sports/baylor-bears/20120309-baylor-s-kim-mulkey-is-fierce-loving-and-loyal-but-dont-get-on-her-bad-side.ece.

"The Immortal Ten." *baylorbears.com: Traditions*. baylorbears.com/trads/bay-immortal-10.html.

Lefever, Alan J. *The History of Baylor Sports*. Waco: Baylor University Press, 2013.

Madden, Lance. "Robert Griffin III, Adidas Have a Lot of Sock Swag." *Forbes*. 21 Sept. 2012. http://www.forbes.com/sites/lancemadden/2012/09/21/robert-griffin-iii-adidas-have-a-lot-of-sock-swag/.

Morgan, Summer. "A Baylor Bearett: Lady Bears Have Come a Long Way Since Sue Turner's Tenure." *MYPlainview.com*. 7 April 2012. http://www.myplainview.com/sports/article.

Moss, Irv. "Colorado Classics: Legacy High Alum Melissa Jones Was an Inspirational Athlete at Baylor." *The Denver Post*. 26 Dec. 2012. http://www.denverpost.com/ci_22259767/legacy-high-alum-melissa-jones-was-an-inspirational-athlete-at-baylor/article.

"Obi Leaps for Bears' 1st National Title Since 2009." *Waco Tribune-Herald*. 16 March 2014. http://www.wacotrib.com/sports/baylor/baylor_track_and_field/obi-leaps-for-bears-st-national-title-since/article.

"Obi Wins NCAA Indoor Triple Jump Crown." *baylorbears.com*. 15 March 2014. http://www.baylorbears.com/sports/c-track/recaps/031514aab.html.

Olson, Max. "Baylor Finds Breakout Weapon in Norwood." *ESPN.com*. 19 Nov. 2013. http://www.espn.go.com/blog/ncfnation/post/_/id/8865t4/baylor-finds-breakout-weapon-in-norwood.

Orts, Jason. "Lady Bears Freshman Nina Davis Overlooked No More." *Waco Tribune-Herald*. 9 Feb. 2014, http://www.wacotrib.com/sports/baylor/lady_bears_basketball/lady-bears-freshman-nina-davis-overlooked-no-more/a rticle.

Parchman, Will. "K-State's Heisman, BCS Title Hopes Cast Aside." *Waco Tribune-Herald*. 18 Nov. 2012. http://www.wacotrib.com/sports/baylor/will-parchman-k-state-s-heisman-bcs-hopes-cast/article.

-----. "Ludy Saves Bears from Epic Collapse." *Waco Tribune-Herald*. 20 March 2011. http://www.wacotrib.com/sports/baylor/ludy-saves-bears-from-epic-collapse/article.

Pond, David. "Seeing the Light." *Sharing the Victory Magazine*. MarchApril 2012. http://archives.fca.org/vsItemDisplay.

"Program History." *2013 Baylor Football Media Almanac*. http://www.baylorbears.com/sports/m-footbl/13-media-almanac.html.

"Robert Griffin III." *baylorbears.com*.http://www.baylorbears.com/sports/m-footbl/mtt/griffiniiirobert00.html.

Schlabach, Mark. "Briles' Offense Built Around Each QB." *ESPN*. 16 Oct. 2013. http://espn.go.com/college-football/story/_/id/9833069/baylor-coach-art-briles-builds-offense-quarterback.

Shamik, Morton. "A Coach Even the Faculty Likes." *Sports Illustrated*. 18 Nov. 1963. http://www.sportsillustrated.cnn.com/vault/article/magazine/MAG1075384/index.htm.

Sherrington, Kevin. "Late Mickey Sullivan Kept Baylor on Top with Casual Style. *Dallas Morning news*. 31 March 2012.

http://www.dallasnews.com/sports/columnists/kevin-sherrington/20120331-sherrington-late-mickey-sullivan-kept-baylor-on-top-with-casual-style.ece.

Teaff. Grant. "2 Seasons That Changed Baylor Football Forever." *Waco Tribune-Herald*. 22 Sept. 2013. http//www.wacotrib.com/sports/baylor/football/grant-teaff-seasons-that-changed-baylor-football-forever/article.

-----. "1980 Team Turned Setback into a Comeback." *Waco Tribune-Herald*. 28 Oct. 2013. http://www.wacotrib.com/sports/baylor/football/grant-teaff-remembers-team-turned-setback-into-a-comeback/article.

-----. "Confident Bears Showed the Difference in '72." *Waco Tribune-Herald*. 7 Sept. 2013. http://www.wacotrib.com/sports/baylor/football/grant-teaff-confident-bears-showed-the-difference-in/article.

-----. "Final Games End But Memories Last." *Waco Tribune-Herald*. 7 Dec. 2013. http://www.wacotrib.com/sports/baylor/football/grant-teaff-remembers-final-games-end-but-memories-last.

-----. "Higher Stakes Yield Cheers at 'Big House.'" *Waco Tribune-Herald*. 5 Oct. 2013. http://www.wacotrib.com/sports/baylor/football/grant-teaff-remembers-higher-stakes-yield-cheers-at-big-house/article.

-----. "Memories Extend Beyond Field of Play." *Waco Tribune-Herald*. 7 Nov. 2013. http://www.wacotrib.com/sports/baylor/football/grant-teaff-memories-extgend-beyond-field-of-play/article.

-----. "Step of Faith Led to Most Unexpected Landing Spot." *Waco Tribune-Herald*. 31 Aug. 2013. http://www.wacotrib.com/sports/baylor/football/grant-teaff-step-of-faith-led-to-most-unexpected-landing-spot/article.

-----. "Wriggly Stunt Helps 1978 Baylor Team Turn Corner." *Waco Tribune-Herald*. 12 Oct. 2013. http://www.wacotrib.com/sports/baylor/football/grant-teaff-wriggly-stunt-helps-baylor-team-turn-corner/article.

Torre, Pablo S. "Back of All Trades." *Sports Illustrated*. 26 Sept. 2011. htttp://www.sportsillustrated.cnn.com/vault/article/magazine/MAG1190636/index.htm.

Ubben, David. "Baylor Continuing to 'Shock' the World." *FoxSports.com*. 12 Nov. 2013, http://www.msn.foxsports.com/southwest/story/baylor-continuing-to-shock-the-world-111213.

Wahl, Grant. "Choice Words." *Sports Illustrated*. 12 Dec. 2005. http://www.sportsillustrated.cnn.com/vault/article/magazine/MAG1114641/index.htm.

Watkins, Calvin. "Ordeal Brings Blackmon Sisters Closer." *Dallas Morning News*. 3 April 2005.

Werner, John. "Afterword" Redefining Unbelievable." *Year of the Bear: The Winningest Year in College Sports History*. Waco: Pediment Publishing, 2012. 139-142.

-----. "Baylor Legend Elkins Helped Shape Future of College Football, Gets Hall of Fame Nod." *Waco Tribune-Herald*. 14 Nov. 2009. http://www.wacotrib.com/sports/baylor/football/baylor-legend-elkins-helped-shape-future-of-college-football/article.

-----. "Baylor Men Knock Off No. 3 Crfeighton, 85-55, to advance to Sweet 16. *Waco Tribune-Herald*. 24 March 2014. http://www.wacotrib.com/sports/baylor/mens_basketball/baylor-men-knock-off-no-creighton-to-advance/article.

-----. "Baylor Receiver Lets Game Do His Talking." *Waco Tribune-Herald*. 15 Oct. 2010. http://www.wacotrib.com/sports/baylor/baylor-receiver-lets-game-do-his-talking/article.

-----. "Bears Rein in Mustangs with Solid Defensive Effort. *Waco Tribune-Herald*. 3 Sept. 2012. http://www.wacotrib.com/sports/football/baylor/bears-rein-in-mustangs-with-solid-defensive-effort/article.

-----. "Bowl Eligibility Only Footnote as Bears Dismantle Cyclones 71-7." *Waco Tribune-Herald*. 20 Oct. 2013. http://www.wacotrib.com/sports/baylor/football/bowl-eligibility-only-footnote-as-bears-dismantle-cyclones/article.

-----. "DE McAllister Showing Doubters Wrong at Baylor." *Waco Herald-Tribune*. 5 Oct. 2013. http://www/wacotrib.com/sports/football/de-mcallister-showing-doubters-wrong-at-baylor/article.

-----. "Floyd Casey's 1st Tenants Share Tales of 1950 Triumphs." *Waco Tribune-Herald*. 31 Aug. 2013. http://www.wacotrib.com/sports/baylor/football/floyd-casey-s-st-tenants-share-tales-of-triumphs/article.

-----. "Hall of Fame Profile: All-AmericanQB Don Trull Took Leap of Faith with Baylor." *Waco Tribune-Herald*. 24 Jan. 2014. http://wwwwacotrib.com/sports/baylor/football/hall-of-fame-profile-all-american-qb-don-trull/article.

-----. "Last Year's Baylor Comeback Over Kansas Still Boggles the Mind." *Waco Tribune-Herald*. 2 Nov. 2012. http://www.wacotrib.com/sports/baylor/john-werner-last-year-s-comeback-over-kansas/article.

-----. "New Baylor Linebacker Showing He Only Needed Chance." *Waco Tribune-Herald*. 14 Sept. 2012. http://www.wacotrib.com/sports/baylor/new-baylor-linebacker-showing-he-only-needed-chance/article.

-----. "Robert Griffin III Wins Baylor's First Heisman Trophy." *Year of the Bear: The Winningest Year in College Sports History*. Waco: Pediment Publishing, 2012. 25-27.

-----. "Trophy Case." *Waco Tribune-Herald*. 8 Dec. 2013. http://www.wacotrib.com/sports/baylor/football/trophy-case-bears-brave-bitter-cold-for-big-title-bcs/article/.